THE FANTASTIC
ELASTIC
BRAIN

THE FANTASTIC
ELASTIC
BRAIN

How to Empower Your Child's Mind

BETSY SCHOOLEY

Published 2018
Printed in the United States of America
Print ISBN: 978-0-9995659-0-2
E-ISBN: 978-0-9995659-1-9
Library of Congress Control Number: 2018904270

Cover and interior design by Tabitha Lahr

For information, address: Betsy@FantasticElasticBrain.com

I dedicate this book to
my sister, Jeanbrown Schooley,
who spent the last years of her
life in my home, encouraging
me to write this book.

And to
Donna L. Morrish, LMFT
who was the instigator of
this book, and then my number-one
cheerleader throughout the process.

CONTENTS

Preface

I STARTED TEACHING IN 1970, and in the years since, I've taught in almost every grade, kindergarten through eighth. I worked in California's Bay Area—in Richmond, Oakland, and San Francisco—before moving to Guatemala to learn Spanish in order to acquire a California bilingual teaching certificate.

I was teaching in the American School of Guatemala in February 1976 when a massive, 7.6 earthquake destroyed countless villages and killed thousands of people. Because my school was closed for four months, I worked in earthquake relief. The culmination of my relief work was the reconstruction of a small school in the town of San Cristobal el Alto, near Antigua. I helped to raise money for building materials through my network of friends and colleagues back in the United States.

The men of the town cut the trees for the wood and manually machined cement blocks one at a time. They built the school themselves, and I was honored to have the school named for me: the Betsy Schooley School (Escuela Nacional Rural Mixta Betsy Schooley). This experience taught me about profound motivation, and I discovered that I found absolute joy in helping others. I felt worthwhile and useful during the relief effort. This was the most fulfilling time of my life.

I eventually moved back to San Francisco to teach and earn my master's degree. In 1981, I moved east to pursue a job in television sports production. This led me to work in New York, Boston, and ultimately Champaign, Illinois, where I was born and raised and where my family still lived.

The birth of my daughter in August 1988 was the catalyst for a lot of pondering and decision making about my two professions. That year I taught English as a Second Language at an elementary school in Champaign. Those ESL classes, with students from ten countries, were rewarding, and being back in Champaign returned to my mind the values with which I grew up, as well as the many discussions I'd had over the years with my Champaign high school teacher-mentor, Louise Walczak. Louise had instilled in me that teaching gave people the opportunity to change lives, and I had indeed experienced that power as a teacher myself. I decided that year that I would rather make a difference in children's lives than televise people in sporting events.

In 1989, as a single mom, I moved back to the Bay Area, which I believed would be an easier place to raise my daughter. I continued teaching, which included seven years in Hayward Spanish bilingual classes.

Then, in the late '90s and early 2000, a confluence of events transpired to uncover a diagnosis of ADHD for me. While I was aware that it was difficult to track multiple streams of information while under stress, what I hadn't realized was that this was part of an ongoing side effect of my brain's tendency to go offline when overstimulated.

At this time in my life, there were competing challenges in my job assignment, and I was receiving less than adequate support. You might say it was a perfect storm. I was assigned a third-and-fourth-grade class in which more than half the fourth-graders were unable to read at grade level. In addition, I was charged with teaching the fourth-grade curriculum books (which they could not read) and preparing for the state tests. Even though I had many years in the classroom, I had always taught children, not the book! There was also daily checking up on my classroom, which was the tipping point for me; my ability to sort, track, focus, and follow through when demands on me were multiple and unmitigated was limited.

While feelings of overwhelm were what led me to therapy, it was the diagnosis that inspired me to begin to systematically identify how I could alleviate some of the symptoms. I met with a therapist to learn about ADHD in adulthood and developed new empathy for my young students who had been labeled as ADD or ADHD. I read every book and magazine article I could find on the subject. I attended a weekend ADD women's conference near Seattle. I realized that some of the quirks I had thought were just part of my personality were actually symptoms of ADHD that were affecting my quality of life.

In 2004, when I was fifty-five, I retired early from the classroom. I wish I had known then what I know now about the brain. I left the classroom with a mixture of sadness and relief. I was relieved that I would not have to fight bureaucratic battles anymore, and sad that the nature of teaching had changed so much, as well as that my last year had been filled with stressors I did not understand, including the fact that I felt neither my students nor I had been successful that school year.

When I was discussing ADHD with a friend one day after I retired, she recommended I call Vickie Bockenkamp, of Power Tools for Learning, to ask for help with my ADHD. Vickie assessed me and explained to me that the left hemisphere of my brain was shut down. She performed a number of activities to "open up" the nonworking parts, a lot of which involved physical touch on various acupressure points. I called this the Vickie Protocol. When she finished, Vickie declared that my left hemisphere had a pulse. I have since used the same approach to elicit a pulse in my own clients.

As my brain opened up, my ability to think and problem-solve improved, and my view of myself was altered. I was also intrigued by what Vickie was accomplishing with kids. And then she recommended a book that changed the course of my postretirement life: Dr. Charles Krebs's *A Revolutionary Way of Thinking*, a book that focuses on the brain's plasticity.

I read Krebs's book three times, and each time it further illuminated for me all of the possibilities that brain plasticity offered. In the book, he discusses factors that cause a loss of brain integration, followed by techniques that help combat such loss. He writes of a man who read aloud falteringly, pausing often, displaying very poor fluency, and revealing poor comprehension. Then he was treated with applied kinesiology, applying pressure on the acupuncture points on the deltoid muscle. While this was happening, he was instructed to move his eyes vertically, horizontally, and near to far. After the application, the man read fluently and had comprehension. This sounded similar to what Vickie had done with me, as well as what I subsequently learned in Touch for Health training, developed by John Thie in the '70s to allow everyday people to use the body's meridians and chakras to improve their health and well-being.

In 2004, knowledge of the brain's plasticity was burgeoning. I absorbed everything I could on the topic, from books like Sharon Begley's *Train Your Mind, Change Your Brain: How a New Science Reveals Our Extraordinary Potential to Transform Ourselves* to Norman Doidge's *The Brain That Changes Itself* and by auditing a University of California, Berkeley, class on neurobiology.

I also returned to Vickie to learn more about helping kids. She offered a Structure of Intellect (SOI) Systems course, in which I learned the basics of SOI and earned a certificate of merit. At the time of this book's publication, I have progressed through the intermediate and advanced levels of SOI training. My clients work on modules from the SOI repertoire nearly every time I have a session with them.

I also studied with Dr. Frank Belgau, who developed equipment—including a pendulum, targets on a target stand, a Platform Balance Board, a Visual Motor Control Stick, and a Rotation Board—for his Learning Breakthrough Program. Brain plasticity is at work every time a child or adult uses the equipment as Dr. Belgau directs in his manuals and tapes. It is still the focus of my work and my physical office, as children are balancing, challenging their vestibular, and performing intricate movements that increase neurons and neural pathways.

In late 2004, I also opened an office in Castro Valley, California, and was thrilled to be able to share my passion for helping people reconnect with their mental, emotional, and physical/sensory process. I called my business Brain Ways. My first three clients were second-grade boys who displayed ADHD characteristics.

That summer, Dr. Krebs came to the United States to present a talk and a workshop at the fortieth National Touch for Health Kinesiology Conference. I flew to North Carolina to meet him and to take a two-day workshop, led by Brendan O'Hara, on primitive and postural reflexes. I met John Thie of Touch for Health and subsequently studied his program with his son, Matthew Thie, for three weekend sessions in Los Angeles. I immediately incorporated reflex testing and remediation and Touch for Health (TFH) into Brain Ways.

By 2008, my daughter was in college and I had returned to live and work in Guatemala. My SOI assessment revealed possible low visual skills in three clients who I felt needed a COVD optometrist exam and probably vision therapy. Jose Miguel, who you will read about in Chapter 3, went to Florida for two months of VT. For the two teenagers, I needed to learn as much about vision therapy as I could so I could help them to improve their visual skills in my office in Guatemala. Again, I read what I could about vision therapy. I also traveled to Southern California to observe and learn about vision therapy at the offices of two COVD optometrists. I bought equipment and returned to Guatemala to help my low-visual-skills learners there.

In late 2009, when I returned to the States, I continued Brain Ways in Alameda, California. I also began working with students part-time for Gemstone Foundation and as a vision therapist at Larkspur Landing Optometry, and taking classes in vision therapy at COVD conferences. I discovered that many children who are diagnosed with ADHD actually have vision binocularity problems and learned how to guide them to improve their visual skills, with great success.

I had also learned from Vickie about brain-changing music. At Brain Ways, I used the Listening Program (TLP) for the first few years. Then, in 2009, I attended practitioner training courses at Integrated Listening Systems (iLs), and since then I've had my clients listen to iLs—on an iPod in my office, and sometimes using the rental program for the home.

Diego and Miguel were thirteen and fourteen years old when they began reading in earnest in Brain Ways. Abbie, who wouldn't wear underclothing and kicked off all of her shoes because they were too "itchy," overcame her sensitivities. Sebastian had none of the twelve primitive and postural reflexes when he arrived. He integrated all of them. Thomas had a fluency score of 67 words per minute when he entered third grade in September, and he zoomed to 102 words per minute by March, as he completed vision therapy. Nate had esotropia. He saw double nearly all the time when he started vision therapy but graduated VT with clear, comfortable binocular vision, no longer seeing double.

This book is a culmination of my personal, teaching, and private-practice experience. I studied. I learned. I tried things on kids. They worked. The amazing results my clients have achieved have been so inspiring that I want to share "how-tos" to bring about change through exercising or activating the brain. I hope to reach parents and teachers who have kids struggling in school in any number of areas—kids who will thrive as a result of rewiring their brain through the activities in the chapters that follow. Every child—and adult, for that matter—can indeed change their brain and change their life.

Introduction

I READ THE BOOK *The Power of Now.*

I sang the song "The Power of One."

I used "The Power of X" to integrate the left and right hemispheres of the brain.

If people everywhere would use "The Power of X," their brains would work more efficiently.

Just looking at an X, drawing an X, *thinking* of an X, or completing an infinity sign (also known as Lazy 8 or an Active 8, which contains an X in the middle) activates both sides of the brain. It is a *powerful*, amazing tool.

Imagine this scene: An eighth grader, his mom, and his grandma are each standing with an arm held out in front of them for a muscle test. (Muscle testing is a kind of body biofeedback. Muscle testing can check the body's response to stimuli by applying pressure to a muscle before and after introducing some sensory information, and then assessing the body's energetic and subtle neurological response through changes in the muscle's strength.)

I walk to each arm and show each person the difference between "hold," "let it go," and "fight me so I can't push your arm down." I check to see if the arm holds when I try to push it down softly with two fingers. Each of the three holds their arm firmly when I ask them to, as I push gently. Then I hold up a paper with two black, parallel lines and ask each person to look at the lines for ten seconds. Then I ask each in turn to hold their arm firmly as I prepare to push gently. As I push gently, each arm goes down to the side for each and every one of them. Each person knows they were trying to hold their arm up, and yet I pushed it down easily. Why? Because the two parallel lines separated the two hemispheres of the brain so they could not "talk" to each other.

I then show them a drawing of a large X and muscle-test them again. As I muscle-test them, they are successful; when I push each arm, it shows "easy to hold" or "locked." The children, their relatives, and their friends are so surprised that just by their looking at an X, they allow their brain to integrate. Both sides can once again "talk" to each other.

You might rightfully say that you do not normally look at two parallel lines. And I agree. However, there are many instances in life that cause our brain hemispheres to lose communication: specifically, when we are under stress. Parents might not be aware when their children are in stress mode. However, children experience stress in their day-to-day lives: when a parent yells at them, when a teacher calls on them to read aloud, when they are crossing a street. These are all stressful situations that might cause the hemispheres to lose communication and the child to operate at less than full potential.

This one explanation of the brain and its workings is something that every teacher all over the world could use as a way to prepare students to learn. I encourage my learners to watch the pencil point as they draw, in the air or on paper, an X or Lazy 8/Active ∞ whenever they need brain power. Unfortunately, how the brain works and how to optimize it for learning are rarely taught in teacher-preparation courses (with the exception of Russia and Germany).

You must be very careful if you check your child with the following two pages. I am including a full page X as well as a full page with two parallel lines so you can show your child how the X works. You might consult the book *Touch for Health* by John Thie to be sure you are checking the muscle correctly. After you test the muscle with the parallel lines it is imperative to then do the X last, so the two hemispheres can reintegrate.

CHAPTER 1:

Brain Gym/Educational Kinesiology

WHEN I READ DR. CARLA HANNAFORD'S book *Smart Moves: Why Learning is Not All in Your Head*, I was amazed by her stories of changes made by her students. She wrote of a ten-year-old girl who barely spoke in sentences and had yet to start reading. After a few months of Hannaford implementing Brain Gym/Educational Kinesiology with the girl, the child's parents came to school to investigate what she had been doing, as she had changed so much! The little girl was now able to read and write for the first time. Hannaford also wrote of a soccer team she worked with. At the end of their championship game's first half, the kids decided they were not communicating well with each other or playing at the level they knew they possessed. Hannaford had taught them many Brain Gym activities, and they chose to lie down on the ground and try one of them: Hook-ups.

Many of Hannaford's stories made sense to me, and I wanted to see if my clients could achieve similar results, so I immediately began studying Brain Gym.

Brain Gym was developed by Paul Dennison, PhD, in the 1970s, and refined and expanded during the '80s and beyond with his wife, Gail. Brain Gym is a series of simple movement activities that cross the body's midline, thus sending neural information from the right-side body movements to the left hemisphere of the brain and left-side body movements to the right hemisphere. As the name implies, Brain Gym is a series of sensorimotor activities that "switch on" the brain (Dennison & Dennison 2010). Just as muscles grow and become stronger in the body through weight training and physical exercise, the brain's neurons and neural pathways are activated with Brain Gym. Connections are made left-right, right-left, front-back, back-front, top-bottom and bottom-top—every way that movement can go, a path can also go.

Metaphor is a powerful way for learners to understand their learning challenges. In *The Learning Gym: Fun-to-Do Activities for Success at School,* Erich Ballinger writes, "Brain Gym integrates the two sides of the brain for whole-brain learning. This integration is necessary because—at any age—stress, fear of failure, and a lack of self-confidence may cause one half of the brain to overwork and the other half to 'switch itself off.' We are then working to only half of our potential, and for a child, this can lead to failure at school" (2004, 7).

You can study this method by reading the many books on Educational Kinesiology and Brain Gym written by the Dennisons and others. In addition, Brain Gym/Educational Kinesiology Workshops are offered all over the United States and internationally by qualified Brain Gym instructors. I will include a picture and a brief description of the activities I use most often with my clients/learners at the end of this chapter in action guide–like form, so parents and teachers can begin to guide their children in immediately discovering how to better move to integrate new learning.

The cortex of the human brain has been mapped. Here is a description from Dr. Charles Krebs and a figure that might help you understand:

> In the 1940s and '50s the neurosurgeon Wilder Penfield mapped much of the brain using electrical stimulation of the brains of conscious patients during brain surgery. Achieved with the cooperation of patients undergoing brain surgery, the process allowed him to take a very close look at some localised areas that seem to be very strongly related to function. Because brain tissue has no pain receptors, the skull can be opened while a person is under a local anesthetic and fully conscious. In this way scientists have been able to insert fine electrodes into specific parts of the brain, stimulate these areas with a mild electric current and ask the patient what they feel (Krebs 1998).

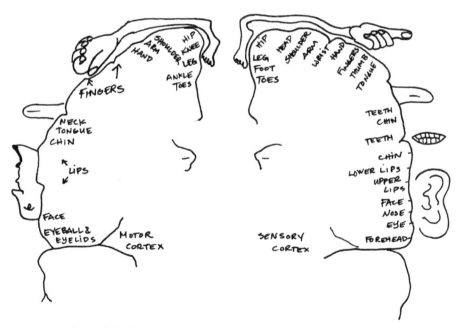

Drawing by Sarah Graff

This topographic representation of motor and sensory function, with body regions drawn as proportional to the area of motor or sensory cortex devoted to that body part, really helped me understand how important movement of body parts is to developing the brain. The emphases on hands, feet, ear, and face became even more relevant to me as I learned Brain Gym, Belgau Learning Breakthrough, Structure of Intellect, Integrated Listening Systems, and all the rest of the systems I use in Brain Ways.

Dr. Krebs continues, "All of this makes complete sense because obviously, it would require more brain cells to operate a function that requires finer motor skills or interpret more precise sensory perception. The greater the degree of motor function or sensory perception at a particular area of the body, the greater is the space it takes up in the brain" (Krebs 1998).

Now, the idea of neuroplasticity—the brain's ability to reorganize itself by forming new neural connections throughout life—is accepted. Now, knowledge of the brain's workings is in magazines and TV news. And now, the various brain scans that can be completed—positron emission tomography (PET), single-photon emission computed tomography (SPECT), and functional magnetic resonance imaging (fMRI)—show *that even thinking of movement causes neurons to fire, which shows the relationship of body parts to areas of the brain.*

Every time I reflect on the value of motion/movement in the classroom, I cannot help but chuckle about Dedric, a whirlybird kindergarten student in 1989. Whenever we had listening time on the rug—usually when I was reading a story to the class or giving instructions—Dedric would place himself in the back, just off the rug, and spin on his shoulder, going in circles, pushing with his feet. And Dedric's memory for what had transpired during "rug time" was flawless. He could repeat verbatim the story or instructions every time I checked. I realize now that the movement cemented the learning in his brain. Too bad the rest of the "good little boys and girls" sat quietly!

Every client with whom I work in Brain Ways, no matter their age, starts their day with PACE, which stands for Positive, Active, Clear, and Energetic (Dennison & Dennison 2010). The actions provide oxygen to the brain, for better functioning, and integrate the right and left hemispheres (Water, Oxygen, Cross Crawl, Hook-ups, and Lazy 8s /Active 8s). PACE helps you in the moment, giving you an opportunity to focus. The PACE acronym goes in a circle, so in the list below it appears to be backward. What is important is that as you prepare to learn, the relaxed, unstressed, self-initiated pace allows for optimal learning (2010, 27). The activities that follow are from Brain Gym's PACE:

- **E Energetic** (Water): Drink water to hydrate.
- **C Clear** (Oxygen): Send oxygen through the blood throughout the brain, choosing the Ear/Thinking Caps, Energy/Lion Yawn, or Brain Buttons.
- **A Active** (Cross Crawl): Complete at least five minutes of the Cross Crawl.
- **P Positive** (Hook-ups): Neural pathways are geared up with Hook-ups.

As I mentioned in the preface, I started my Brain Ways business in 2004 in Castro Valley, California. My first clients were three second graders. Each boy was, of course, different from the next, but all three had been labeled as having attention deficit hyperactivity disorder (ADHD), either by teachers or by educational psychologist testing.

When I started doing the Brain Gym Cross Crawl with Jay, age seven, he could not sustain the crossing. He would touch his left hand to his left leg and his right hand to his right leg. He had midline processing issues. I went right to work incorporating Brain Gym exercises. If his parent or I watched closely, we could redirect Jay when he returned to his one-sided, ipsilateral way of doing the Cross Crawl, so that he was eventually doing the Cross Crawl correctly most of the time. (Dennison & Dennison, 2010) Jay also benefited from doing a lot of rolling up within a rug for sensory integration, as well as vestibular challenges on various balance boards.

Paul was nearing the end of second grade when he began his sessions with me. He completed his work with me in a small room in his school. Hook-ups seemed to have a very calming effect on Paul, who I had seen act out in my office. As a second-grader, Paul had flunked most of his weekly spelling tests throughout the year. On the third week of doing Brain Gym with me, his teacher showed me his weekly test, on which he had misspelled only one word.

"I wish you had been working with him all year," she said, "as most of his spelling tests were illegible and often showed no phonics relationships between letter and sound."

Paul continued to improve his behavior and academics in his class.

Dee had been labeled ADHD by his teacher, and his parents had received many complaints that he did not pay attention in class. It turned out that Dee had sensory integration issues, specifically central auditory processing disorder. Testing showed that Dee did not process what he heard in his left ear if there was any noise at all in his right. It seemed incredible to me that Brain Gym could help Dee. However, in Paul Dennison's work, he has written of the improvements he's observed in visual and auditory processing by students who do the Brain Gym exercises regularly, so Dee and I performed them at least twice a week when we had sessions, and I asked him to complete PACE with Active 8s each day at home.

As I continued with more students at Brain Ways, I felt that each learner with whom I worked benefited from doing Brain Gym. Then I moved to Guatemala for three years and found the same results. As the years have passed, I have worked with children in both countries and have always been impressed at the changes my learners show.

As a matter of course, I advise all of my clients to complete ten to fifteen minutes of Brain Gym a day, preferably before and during school.

I fondly remember one client in particular, Sebastian. Whenever he would see me at his school, Sebastian would proudly march past me, touching the opposite knee with the opposite hand, and say, "I did all my exercises this morning before school, Ms. Betsy." As you will read in Chapter 2, "Retained Primitive and Postural Reflexes," Sebastian integrated his reflexes in less than four months; I believe that this was specifically because he practiced his exercises daily.

The benefits of Brain Gym activities were especially highlighted during my visits to an orphanage outside of Guatemala City. Sadly, there were a substantial number of orphans in Guatemala. At the orphanage I visited, there was a school on the property as well. I delivered a workshop on Brain Ways, retained reflexes, Brain Gym, and vision therapy (VT) to the staffs of both institutions. It was extremely enjoyable, as the teachers and house parents were totally engaged. I anticipated that numerous children were going to be able to overcome a variety of difficulties with help from those present.

I next visited the orphanage to work with the teachers and five groups of students. The groups varied from each other in distinct ways. I engaged all the groups in my Brain Gym favorites for integrating the hemispheres for ADHD kids. Then we participated in a variety of songs, activities, and brain-bag actions from Brendan O'Hara's *Movement & Learning* CDs. I am not sure if you can appreciate, without actually being there, the creativity of twenty boys, at ten years old, doing their Active 8s with brain bags to the song "Under the Leg and in the Air" (O'Hara 2003a). The idea is to envision an Active 8 and complete one in the air with a bag in hand, watching with binocularity—both eyes binocularly focused in the midfield.

What was supposed to happen in that group, and what actually happened, were two different things. I think the boys took "in the air" to mean "throw the brain bag as hard and fast as I can under my leg to hit the guy next to me!" It took some art to throw the brain bag and most definitely some skill to catch a "missile" coming from another boy. I have to admit that I found this group to be my favorite. All twenty boys were full of energy, and we could generally get through twice as many songs as I could with any other group.

This group also contained the most kids who would say to me, "Doña Betsy, I practice my 8s on the ceiling every night."

So I knew they were learning and growing their brains as well as having fun.

The special-needs group at the orphanage showed the most improvement over the months. I believe it might be due to the fact that these children had probably all been neglected for so long before they reached the orphanage. Each Brain Gym activity we did seemed to establish new sensorimotor habits and neural pathways.

This group worked at a slow pace. Some of the children had been diagnosed with physical disabilities, some with mental difficulties, and some were identified as having both. I decided it was important to engage each of these special-needs children in Dennison Laterality Repatterning (Dennison and Dennison 2010). In this case, however, this simple process came with some challenges. When I tried to perform Cross Crawl with the whole group, almost all the children reverted to ipsilateral movement. I would position myself in front of a child in order to direct his hand to come across and touch his opposite knee. Unfortunately, the cross-lateral rhythm would last for only about three repetitions, and then the child's hands would go back to touching the same-sided knee. There was a lot of redirection and one-on-one learning in this group.

In addition to my work at the orphanage, I presented a workshop to the teachers at the school near my apartment in the capital. In each classroom I was invited into, I asked that the teacher stay to learn each Brain Gym movement that I used with the students. I would make a big Active 8 on chart paper and hang it above the chalkboard, or else I would just draw one on the board. The class would stand, face the Active 8 with a thumb in the air, and follow the Active 8 around five times with one hand, five with the other, and then five times with the two thumbs together. Then we would perform the Thinking Cap, Lion Yawn/Energy Yawn or Brain Buttons, followed by the Cross Crawl and Hook-ups (Dennison & Dennison 2010).

The students were always disappointed when I gathered up the brain bags to take to the next class after we did the songs and chants from Brendan O'Hara's CDs (2003a, 1991) with them. First one inventive teacher, then another, and then nearly all of them assigned their students a homework assignment of sewing a small, square bag filled with rice. Soon, every student had their brain bag on the desk when I entered.

There were variations of the orphanage boys' fun with the bags, as the classrooms had the old, hanging lights (large rectangles, hanging down about two feet from the ceiling). Sometimes, while performing to the O'Hara chants, a wayward brain bag would "diddly bom bom shew" or "rainbow, rainbow" all the way up near the ceiling and land on one of the hanging lamps!

I encouraged the teachers to do the exercises and activities every day, not just when I visited. It was obvious soon thereafter which classes were doing Active 8s and bag activities before their spelling tests and classwork. Various kids would tell me during my visits that they had done well on tests or better on their schoolwork after their exercises. Overall, it was encouraging to witness each and every individual success.

I want to mention the kindergarten class at this Guatemalan school and how we used movement and music or rhythm to really cement learning into the children's brains, even though we were doing only the Cross Crawl from the Brain Gym movements. I spent extra time and days in the kindergarten class because I love the age, the expectancy, and the huge growth in learning visible in kindergarten. I made the decision to utilize the Zoo Phonics Spanish alphabet to engage their brains. In Zoo Phonics, every animal has a name, a picture with the letter of the alphabet embedded into the picture of the animal, and an action that is completed as the sound is emitted. The children were enthralled with the pictures and the animals. Within a week, we could put my little beanie-baby animals on the students' desks, and they could all say the sound and act out the action as each animal was held up.

From there we advanced to the more traditional reading of the Spanish syllables—*sa, se, si, so, su* in "*Susana y su sapo*" and *fa, fe, fi, fo, fu* in "*Felipe es una foca que vive muy feliz*"—in songs from *Cancionero! Big Book of Songs*. The teacher made sure they were performing some actions like clapping or the Cross Crawl while singing the songs. The kids learned each song in a few days and could sing the whole book by the time of their June vacation. These students were definitely going to be ready to advance to the next level of learning!

At Brain Ways, I often had parents asking if I could help their ADHD child to "act more appropriately in school" without taking any medications. Of course, I wished I could just change the school, but changing schools is easier said than done. Instead, I started teaching my clients brain integration. I also helped my learners "adjust" to the school so their lives would be more pleasant and the parents' "fight over homework" could also be relieved. The more I worked my program with ADHD kids, the more success they had in school. This encouraged me to continue incorporating Brain Gym, along with Belgau Platform Balance Board work, The Listening Program (TLP) or Integrated Listening Systems (iLs), Structure of Intellect (SOI), and reflex brain-bags activities, all of which will be referred to in future chapters.

CLIENT SUCCESS

In each chapter of this book, I will include a section entitled "Client Success." In this chapter, Juana, Andre, and Jacob are three examples of children who worked their brain to achieve good results using Brain Gym.

Juana

This extraordinary story comes from a band teacher named Vivian. Juana had joined two of Vivian's bands but was having a hard time mastering the scales. Scales are generally considered easier than sight reading and playing musical pieces. Vivian had planned new music for the group for an upcoming Christmas concert. The scales were played at the beginning of each practice session as the warm-up. Juana had chosen the saxophone as her instrument. Vivian explained to me that there are three sharps in the scales of the saxophone. When she would tell Juana to play one of those sharps—an F sharp, for example—Juana thought she was playing the correct note. She could not tell that her fingers were actually playing an incorrect note.

Vivian was quite concerned. She decided not to single out Juana to do the Brain Gym exercises by herself. Instead, Vivian had the entire orchestra stand and perform two to three minutes of the Cross Crawl in order to support left/right integration for everyone, including Juana. Each time Juana did the Thinking Cap and the Cross Crawl with the other musicians, she would sit back down and play the scales correctly. Vivian considered this a near miracle, so she continued to start each band session with the Cross Crawl.

As Vivian explained to me, sometimes she was running late and would rush in telling her students to play the scales. As soon as she would hear Juana's off-key F sharp, Vivian would remember that she had skipped the Cross Crawl. She would stop the group, asking them to march in place with their hands tapping their opposite knees. Indeed, Juana was "switched off," a descriptive term in applied kinesiology, so Vivian was helping her each and every session!

Andre

A situation involving one of my clients, Andre, exemplifies the importance of Brain Gym's Hook-ups. When the kids practiced Hook-ups with me in the office, I would tell them to perform them every morning before school and during their day, if they felt that they were not thinking optimally. One day Andre told me this story: During an eighth-grade English class, he was taking a test. He became stymied on a question and started to do Hook-ups with his legs outstretched on the side of his desk and his eyes closed.

All of a sudden, the teacher looked at him and asked, "What in the blazes are you doing, Andre?"

He opened his eyes and replied, "Ms. Betsy said that whenever I know I have studied something and I just can't think of it in the moment, to do these Hook-ups so my brain can relax and the answer will come back to me."

The teacher just nodded and retorted that maybe everyone should do Hook-ups like Andre.

Jacob

Brain Gym movements were also essential for another one of my students: five-year-old Jacob, who could not toss a small, rice-filled brain bag from one hand to another. Even when he tried a toss of only two or three inches from one hand to the other, the bag would land on the floor, much to my surprise and his frustration. I began doing some simple, basic Brain Gym movements with Jacob, including Active 8s on the wall. As he had sensory integration dysfunction (SID), Jacob did not like the Cross Crawl; he did not like to touch his knee. So we devised methods where he was mimicking the action of the Cross Crawl and crossing the midline without the physical touch. You can read more about Jacob's success in Chapter 2, "Retained Primitive and Postural Reflexes." He eventually came a long way from those early, frustrating times!

ACTION GUIDE

I remember the TV slogan to join the US Armed Forces: "Be All You Can Be." Every time I would hear these words, I would almost automatically, out loud, add three words: "Do Brain Gym."

Parents can easily do these activities before school with their child. Or, if the parents are already at work doing *Brain Gym for Business* (Dennison, Dennison, and Teplitz 2004), the children can perform the Brain Gym activities on their own on the way to school, whether traveling by car or school bus or walking.

Hydrate: Drink lots of water daily. Brain activity is enhanced with the oxygen in the blood from water.

Brain Buttons: Rub the two indentations below the clavicle with your opened hand, using the index finger and thumb. First, rub clockwise for thirty seconds. Then, rub counterclockwise for another thirty seconds with your other hand held in the same index finger-thumb position. While moving one hand, the opposite hand should be placed over the navel. (Note: This is on the kidney meridian and is a wonderful exercise if you are right-left challenged. Perform Brain Buttons and see how the left-right confusion goes away!)

The Thinking Cap: Place your thumbs on the inside top of your ears and softly pinch outside. Roll the skin of your ear outwards. Move from the top to the bottom of your ear and back up at least three times.

The Energy Yawn (which I often call the Lion Yawn): Place four fingers on the temporomandibular joint (TMJ)—the joint of the jaw on your cheek, just in front of the ear opening. Gently massage both TMJ areas of your face as you open your mouth widely with a quiet "roar" yawn.

The Cross Crawl: Move your feet/legs as if marching. Touch the opposite hand/wrist/elbow to your opposite knee, continuing with the other hand/elbow to the other knee.

Hook-ups: Part One—Cross your right foot over your left foot. Extend your arms out in front of you, with the back of your hands touching. Lift your left hand over your right hand and clasp your hands together. Invert your hands under, and then place them under your chin. Touch the roof of your mouth with your tongue. Breathe in deeply through your nose and out through your mouth. Repeat about ten times, counting a slow six while breathing in your nose, and exhaling slowly for a count of six. Repeat.

Hook-ups: Part Two—When ready, uncross your arms and legs, feet flat on the floor, and touch your fingertips together in front of your chest, continuing to breathe deeply for another minute and while holding the tip of your tongue on the roof of your mouth when you inhale (2010, 27).

Lazy 8s (I like to call this Active 8s): Draw a huge infinity sign. I use chart paper. Put a "Start" dot below the right circle and draw an arrow up to the left. For Active 8s, we always start by going up toward the left, going around the left-side circle counterclockwise, back to the X in the middle, and continuing clockwise around the right circle. I ask my clients to do twenty full 8s, using each hand and then both hands together.

I have a small, stuffed seal nearby for little ones to use to follow the lines, and I redraw the infinity sign smaller for them. In Spanish, we sang a song called "La Foca Feliz," so we used a seal (la foca) and often sang the song as the child moved the seal, with the beat, around the 8s. I also ask that clients keep their eyes on their hand, the seal, or the 8 throughout the exercise to be sure that vision is being activated.

I use three varieties of Active 8s: (1) Elephant 8s, for better balance/ vestibular work, where the student extends his/her arm out like an elephant's trunk and traces the Active 8; (2) Alphabet 8s for better penmanship and flowing thoughts for writing, which work best on a balance board for more vestibular work, as the child draws the Active 8 with their ear on the shoulder of the extended arm; and (3) Active 8s for Vision, which involve the eyes following the thumbs moving in the air, from a distance, without touching the chart paper 8 (Dennison & Dennison 2010).

Other Brain Gym exercises are explained in many books. You can also attend Brain Gym workshops worldwide. See www.braingym.org for a list of available workshops and www.braingym.com to order books, posters, and videos.

CHAPTER 2:

Retained Primitive and Postural Reflexes

IT IS EXTRAORDINARY HOW FEW parents and teachers know about these reflexes. I was just lucky, soon after my early retirement from teaching, to meet and study with Brendan O'Hara, an Australian practitioner of kinesiology and primitive and postural reflexes integration who had spent years working with preschool children in Australia to help integrate those reflexes that were still retained. He made up chants, songs, and actions and then used kinesiology and specific exercises to integrate the reflexes. I subsequently met other practitioners who also checked for retained primitive and postural reflexes. I was surprised when I met a woman who told me that she worked only on children who were born by C-section, because they nearly always had some retained reflexes, as these babies did not get to inhibit their primitive reflexes in any "practice" of coming through the birth canal. I immediately went home and tested my own C-section child.

Reflexes are involuntary movements triggered by head and neck movements and by sensory stimulation, first during the fetal stage and then in young babies. Through these reflexes, infants develop from helpless newborns into walking, talking upright human beings. The reflexes produce movements that the infants "practice" until they learn to perform them at will and voluntarily (O'Hara 2003b, 37). Then the reflex is supposed to "inhibit" or "integrate."

"These early movements are developing and practicing for other, later, more complicated movements and activities. Remember the first few attempts at rolling over from back to stomach with all the rocking on the back, getting ready to roll over? The baby then rolls to a certain point and tumbles onto the tummy, without control. Gradually the baby gains control of this activity. All the movements of rolling, rocking, etc., are stimulating muscles, tendons, and joints and joint receptors. Developing . . . using . . . developing . . . practicing . . . using . . . developing . . . the proprioception . . . growing the central nervous system . . . growing our gross-motor and fine-motor coordination and control" (2003b, 37). The reflexes then "inhibit" as the infant gains control. If they do not inhibit, then the child has retained the reflexes.

Some people in the field use the word "inhibit" when the child "inhibits" or "integrates" the reflex. I will use the terms interchangeably in this chapter. In my personal communication with Brendan O'Hara in 2017, he stated that he had changed some of his terminology since his early publications:

> In the intervening years since publishing Wombat and His Mates, I have evolved my vernacular in respect to the primitive and postural reflexes (PPRs). I no longer use the term "the reflex is inhibited." I prefer the phrase "the reflex is integrated . . . into the body." Similarly, I no longer refer to a "reflex being retained"; I now use the phrase "the reflex is persisting." This language instinctively resonates with me as more clearly conveying exactly what is happening with one or many reflexes.
>
> This change in terminology in no way exhibits any disrespect for Sally Goddard. Indeed, I maintain the deepest respect for and gratitude to her for the benefits I, and countless others, have gained from her immense knowledge and experience, derived from an awesome life's work. Thanks, Sally.
>
> —from a personal conversation with Brendan O'Hara

Because I wrote my chapter before learning of O'Hara's changes, I continue to use the term "retained reflexes."

The residual effects of retained reflexes in an infant, child, or adult can be quite serious. For example, if the tonic labyrinthine reflex (TLR) persists beyond age one, the child or adult may have a propensity for motion sickness or have trouble understanding directions. If the Moro reflex persists, a child or adult may have allergies and lowered immunity (Goddard 2005, 7, 21).

Babies should inhibit most of these reflexes by four to twelve months of age.

In this chapter, I will list the names of the ones I assess. Then I will explain how I assess them, as well as enumerate some of the long-term effects that a person who never inhibited one or more reflexes will experience. In the Action Guides section at the end of the chapter, you will learn about activities to integrate the retained reflex at home.

People sometimes believe that retained primitive and postural reflexes apply only to babies. This is not the case. I have met a number of women who also learned about reflexes later in life and realized that they had been living with the consequences of retained reflexes. One woman in her forties burst into tears when Brendan mentioned that adults who still walk on their toes probably never integrated the TLR, possibly because of a difficult birth. Another woman asked to speak with Brendan because he had mentioned some characteristics of people who had retained the TLR, such as spatial difficulties with a direct impact on the concept of time, as well as giving and receiving directions. She thought he was talking to her.

Later, these women and I were taking turns, crawling and checking each other's right-left hand-leg movements, when Brendan asked us all to watch a woman who was over sixty years old. It looked like her arms and legs were showing the expected left-right-left-right sequence. However, the instructor was down on his hands and knees, pointing to her feet. I had never seen anyone crawl with her feet in the air the way this woman was doing. Brendan explained that most people crawl with the tops of their feet dragging behind their legs, but this woman had never integrated the symmetrical tonic neck reflex (STNR), as evidenced by her keeping her feet off the floor.

Approximate Emergence and Duration of the Primitive and Postural Reflexes

Key
E = emergence
I = integration
* = Primitive Reflex
# = Postural Reflex

PREGNANCY   FIRST YEAR   SECOND YEAR   THIRD YEAR

* Fear Paralysis Reflex E, 5-7 Wks I, 9-12 Wks

* Moro E, 9 Wks I, 2-6 Mths

* Palmar E, 11 Wks I, 2-3 Mths

* Plantar E, 11 Wks I, 2-3 Mths

* Suck Reflex E, 11-12 Wks I, 3-4 Mths

* Rooting Reflex E, 1-12 Wks I, 3-4 Mths

* Asymmetrical Tonic Neck Reflex E, 18 Wks I, 4-6 Mths

* Spinal Galant Reflex E, 18-20 Wks I, 3-9 Mths

* Tonic Labyrinthine Reflex E, 12 Wks I, 6-36 Mths

* Symmetrical Tonic Neck Reflex E, 4-9 Mon I, 9-12 Mths

Vestibular Reflex E, 9 Wks I, Remains for Life

Headrighting Reflexe E, 3-12 Mths I, Remains for Life

Amphibian Reflex E, 4-6 Mths I, Remains for Life

© Brendan O'Hara 2016

I mention these women because if a reflex does not inhibit by age two, the person can travel through life with some "leftovers." Retained primitive and postural reflexes affect us physically and emotionally.

I generally test each of my clients for twelve retained reflexes, no matter what their age. The following is the Order of Development List (O'Hara 2004, 9):

1. FEAR PARALYSIS REFLEX

The first reflex in the list is a withdrawal reflex that emerges in the embryonic stage for protection and self-preservation. "The fear paralysis reflex forms the basis for the development of the reflexes. It is detected not by doing a test but by checking with the mother for her history in pregnancy or childbirth. Ask about significant shock, trauma, or tragedy. If there are significant problems presenting you can assume this reflex online. Notice body/posture, eyes, voice" (O'Hara 2004, 10). If a reflex did not inhibit, this inhibition can then affect any or all of these reflexes that follow.

If this reflex is not inhibited, the characteristics can show up as:

- Excessive fear
- Extreme shyness
- Inability to accept change
- Selective mutism (Goddard 2005, 148)

2. MORO REFLEX

Also known as the startle reflex, the Moro reflex acts as a baby's primitive fight-or-flight reaction. If babies hear a loud noise, see a bright light, or are surprised by a touch, their arms will thrust outward. This reflex should be inhibited by four months of age. To ascertain whether the Moro reflex is integrated in a child or an adult, we use three methods. The scarecrow is a quick test in which I stand behind the child to support them and ask them to lean back. The person's feet should not move when the person falls back while standing like a scarecrow with arms outstretched and feet together. An audible "boo!" should startle the person. The visual test

MORO REFLEX

is a quick hand to the eyes to see whether the person flinches (O'Hara 2004, 12). If the feet move during the scarecrow fall, that is indicative of a nonintegrated Moro reflex. The reflex is likely still retained if the person does not flinch or show a reaction to the auditory surprise.

If the Moro reflex persists in the older child or adult, it can be associated with emotional and social immaturity, such as:

- Physical timidity
- Allergies and lowered immunity
- Dislike of change or surprise; poor adaptability
- Stimulus-bound effect (cannot ignore peripheral stimuli; pays attention to everything; very distractible)
- Hypersensitivity to specific sounds; difficulty with shutting out background noise
- Anxiety; angst
- Some need to control and manipulate (Goddard 2005, 6–7)

3. PALMAR REFLEX (PALM OF HAND)

The palmar reflex is the next to emerge and inhibits by two to three months old. The palmar assists in the coordination of fingers and thumbs and hand strength for holding and gripping. It also assists with sucking (O'Hara 2004, 14).

There is a direct link between the palmar reflex and feeding in those early months. The palmar reflex can be elicited by sucking movements, in which the action of sucking may cause kneading of the hands in time to sucking movements. This is called the Babkin response.

When I test children or adults, if there is movement of the fingers,

PALMAR REFLEX

thumb, or mouth area when I gently stroke a person's palm from the out-side to the center, then the palmar reflex did not inhibit at the two-to-three-month stage.

If the palmar fails to inhibit at the correct time, there can be a last-ing effect upon fine-muscle coordination, speech, and articulation, which may include:

- Poor manual dexterity
- Poor "pincer" (pencil) grip when writing
- Speech and articulation difficulties
- Hypersensitivity to tactile stimulation on the palm of the hand
- Mouth movements in children when trying to write or draw (God-dard 2005, 8–9)

4. PRIMITIVE (INFANT) PLANTAR AND BABINSKI REFLEXES

The timing of the emergence of the primitive plantar reflex, also known as the infant plantar or Babinski reflex, often coincides with that of the palmar reflex. The extension part of the reflex is named after the Rus-sian Dr. Babinski, who identified the gesture in which a baby's big toe naturally stretches forward toward their body or the toes curl in, which is useful for babies to grab on to their mothers if they are falling. "The reflex strengthens and coordinates feet and leg muscles in preparation for walking, running, and climbing" (O'Hara 2004, 16). However, when that big toe still extends forward after age two, it is indicative of a retained plantar reflex.

PLANTAR REFLEX

The check for retention of the primitive plantar is similar to the primitive palmar. To determine whether this reflex has been retained, I rub along the sole of the foot. Some people think, *Oh, I'm just ticklish,* but the reflex test is more than that. Any movement in the toes, hands, or mouth area caused by rubbing the sole of the foot can indicate a nonintegrated reflex.

If the reflex is retained, the child or adult may have:

- Ipsilateral (same-sided) walking
- Difficulty running and climbing

5. TONIC LABYRINTHINE REFLEX

The TLR ("tonic" refers to muscles; "labyrinthine" means "like a labyrinth") inhibits gradually and straightens the body after birth. The TLR is essential for vision development. It promotes strength and coordination in the neck, body, and limbs. One of the ways to assess the TLR is to ask the person to lie down and relax, and then to "lightly touch right hand, elbow, shoulder, head, left shoulder, arm/elbow, hand. Then ask

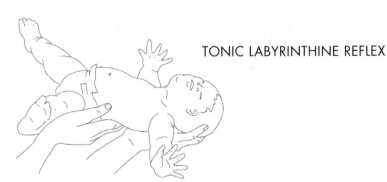

TONIC LABYRINTHINE REFLEX

[the] person to lift everything that you have touched. Do [this with the] person's eyes open, and a few times with their eyes closed" (2004, 18).

Another way to assess this reflex is to have the person tilt their head up and down slowly while sitting with their legs dangling from a table. This tilting can be repeated as a child is lying on their tummy with their feet in the air (2004, 18). If other parts of the body besides the head move while the tilting occurs, the TLR has probably not integrated.

If the TLR persists beyond one year of age, it is often associated with:

- Unsynchronized crawling (rarely crawls on hands and knees)
- Vestibular (propensity to become carsick; poor sense of balance)
- Oculomotor (visual-perceptual difficulties; spatial problems)
- Postural problems, resulting in a child or adult with floppy or tight muscles who may walk on their toes
- Orientation and spatial difficulties, with a direct impact on the subject's concept of time, understanding, and giving directions, or math reasoning
- Dislike of physical education (Goddard 2005, 20–23)

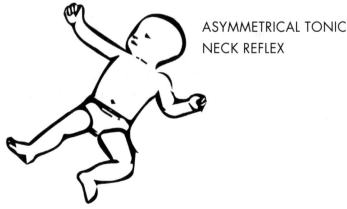

ASYMMETRICAL TONIC NECK REFLEX

6. ASYMMETRICAL TONIC NECK REFLEX

The ATNR is activated as a result of turning the head to one side. As a baby's head is turned, the arm and leg on the same side will extend while the opposite limbs bend. To test for integration in my clients, I have them assume cat position and move their head to determine whether an arm collapses or the angle of the spine changes.

"ATNR facilitates birth [and helps] to develop vision, hand-eye coordination, distance awareness, and balance. ATNR helps generate rolling and ensures a clear breathing passage.

In utero, through 'kicking' [ATNR] develops muscle tone and assists the vestibular" (O'Hara 2004, 20).

If the ATNR remains active in a child at a later age, it can affect all of the below:

- Hand-eye coordination (difficulties such as ability to control the arm and hand when writing, resulting in an awkward pencil grip or turning of the page)
- Lesser standard of writing compared with that which the child can produce orally
- Difficulty with visual tracking (the ability of the eyes to move over and back smoothly along a line of print when reading and writing; child may have to use their finger when reading and may continually lose their place on the page)

- Ability to cross the vertical midline (e.g., a right-handed child may find it difficult to write on the left side of the page; writing may slope one way and then the other)
- Mixed handedness (common in older children and adults) (Goddard 2005, 12)

7. SPINAL GALANT REFLEX

The spinal Galant reflex, which helps babies move through the birth canal and roll over later, is usually inhibited from three to nine months. I check to see whether it has been retained by slowly moving my pointer lightly up and down the back, first about an inch away from the spine and then closer to the side of the body. The pointer moves slowly up from the hip to the shoulder and back again (O'Hara, 2004). If the child or adult squirms or moves back in any way, it signifies a retained spinal Galant.

If the spinal Galant does not inhibit, the symptoms may include:

- Fidgeting
- Bed wetting
- Poor concentration
- Poor short-term memory
- Hip rotation to one side when walking (Goddard 2005, 17)

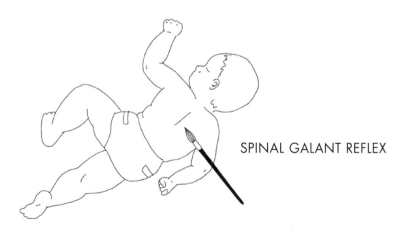

SPINAL GALANT REFLEX

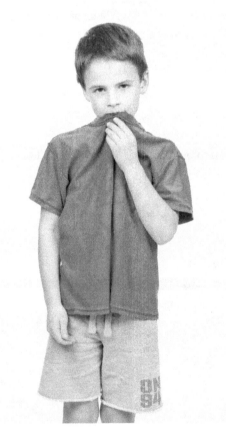

8. SUCKING AND ROOTING REFLEX

The sucking and rooting reflex should be present in all babies who are born at full term. Sucking and rooting are necessary for nourishment, and these reflexes ensure that the baby turns toward the source of the food and opens their mouth. "Produce strength in neck and the mouth. Prepare for speech and aid digestion. Help develop manual dexterity" (2004, 24).

You might have noticed a child who did not get enough sucking and rooting as a baby and did not inhibit at the appropriate time. Have you seen a child over age two who is continually chewing on their shirt collar or sleeve? That is often an indicator of a sucking response that was not inhibited at the normal time of four months.

The actual test for the sucking and rooting reflex in children and adults is to gently stroke with a pointer or paintbrush in four directions, toward the corners of the lips. I find it relatively hard to detect as I touch near their lips. The reaction is often like a short twitch and can be missed. A good rule of thumb is to repeat the test; if the very subtle movement (a partial smile or other movement) is repeated, then it is most likely a reflex.

Long-term effects of retained sucking and rooting reflexes can lead to:

- Hypersensitivity around the lips and mouth
- Difficulty swallowing (the child may dribble and/or need orthodontics)
- Speech and articulation problems brought on by arching of the palate
- Poor manual dexterity (Goddard 2005, 14)

9. SYMMETRICAL TONIC NECK REFLEX

The STNR "teaches the infant to rock and in so doing:

- develops the vestibular system and balance
- introduces our bodies to defying gravity using our own strength
- requires and increases strength in the limbs, spine, muscles, and ligaments

- develops vision, especially binocular focus, both eyes looking at one point
- coordinates balance, vision, and movement" (O'Hara, 2003b, 37)

"Children who retain the STNR (after six to nine months) rarely crawl on hands and knees. They might 'bear walk' on their hands and feet, shuffle on their bottoms, or simply pull themselves up to standing and walk. Those who do crawl may do so in an unusual fashion: The hands may be rotated outward to 'lock' the elbows and/or the feet may be raised. The crawling pattern will be unsynchronized as the timing of the movements in the upper and lower sections of the body do not quite 'match'" (Goddard, 2005, 22, 23).

The STNR is related to eyesight and vision. "Bending of the legs as a result of head extension also encourages the infant to 'fixate' his eyes at far distance. Bending of the arms in response to flexion of the head will bring the child's focus back to near distance, thus training the eyes to adjust from far to near distance and back again" (Goddard 2005, 23).

Have you ever seen a "W" sitter? A "W" sitter is a child who sits with legs and feet out to the side. "W" sitting is the telltale sign of an unintegrated STNR. The young "W" sitter is generally a child who prefers to observe, rather than participate. These children generally have:

- A short attention span and poor concentration, with an inability to focus
- Difficulty with balance
- Poor ball skills (catching is "snatching," with the body very tense)
- Inability to climb back down after climbing up
- Hypermobility in the joints, often with poor posture (O'Hara 2003b)

10. VESTIBULAR REFLEX (BALANCE)

The vestibular reflex is most important for balance, coordination, and sensory integration. A family favorite when I assess for retained reflexes is the vestibular systems test. I generally use a bright object on display from across the width of my office. I ask the client to look at the object, stand on one foot, and count to twenty. Most children and adults can do this without wiggling. However, the vestibular reflex is assessed with the eyes closed. Then one can tell how stable the fluid is in the little vestibular canals in a person's head, especially if the wiggles and jiggles start while counting, "Three, four, five . . ." Kids love it when they can stay still while counting to a higher number than their parent.

Almost every activity that people do in my office challenges the vestibular system, thus strengthening it. I consider the vestibular canals the sentries for the brain. Nothing gets in the brain via vision, taste, smell, touch, or aural senses without passing through the vestibular system. This means that balance, vision, and spatial and body awareness are all closely connected.

If the vestibular remains unintegrated, children may exhibit these characteristics:

- Poor balance and coordination
- Motion sickness
- A lack of aural discrimination, resulting in slow speech development
- Poor short-term memory
- Hyperactivity
- Behavioral problems
- High intelligence, coupled with a lack of focus and poor concentration that make learning difficult (2003b, 36)

11. HEADRIGHTING REFLEX

The headrighting reflex is a postural reflex that facilitates balance, spatial awareness, and coordination. It aids in integrating vision, the vestibular system, and upright posture (2004, 30). It maintains the head in a stable position and the eyes fixed on visual targets, despite other movements of the body, which makes fixation and sustained visual attention possible (Goddard 2005, 33).

Testing the headrighting reflex is fun. Kids love to watch their parents "fail" this simple test in which the client sits on the floor, legs straight

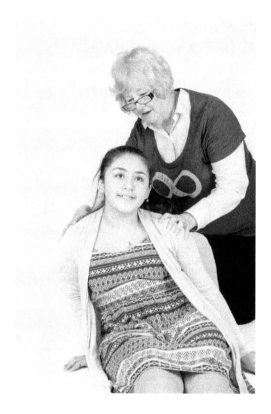

out in front of the body. The client looks at the same bright-colored ball, positioned high in my office, that I use for the vestibular systems check. Then I ask permission to touch the shoulders, and, while the client is watching the object, I move the body forward, backward, and to each side. Someone with an integrated headrighting reflex will keep their head upright, even as their body is tilted to the left or right. In other words, the head is not supposed to move in the direction of the lowered shoulder. If the reflex is retained, however, then the head will not remain upright; it will follow the shoulder toward the ground.

If the headrighting reflex does not inhibit, it may affect:

- Visual fixation
- Visual pursuit
- Reading ability, comprehension, and spelling (Goddard 2005, 33)

12. AMPHIBIAN REFLEX (CRAWLING LIKE A CROCODILE)

The amphibian reflex is intended to facilitate crawling and creeping and to gain body movement independent of the neck and head position. This reflex usually develops at four to six months. As it develops, the ATNR is being inhibited. This inhibition permits the independent movement of the legs and arms, which are essential for crawling, creeping, and gross-motor muscle coordination later on, and enables the child to move one quadrant of the body independently of the other three (Goddard 2005, 34).

To check it, I ask the client to crawl like a crocodile, or "army style," so the learner will drag their belly on the floor while moving the right hand and left leg/foot forward together, and vice versa. Those who do not have the amphibian reflex integrated will be unable to crawl in this oppositional fashion.

An underdeveloped amphibian reflex:

- Will impede cross-pattern crawling and creeping
- May contribute to hypertonus in later life
- May interfere with gross-motor muscle coordination in sports and physical education
- Suggests uninhibited primitive reflexes (Goddard 2005)

CLIENT SUCCESS

Juana

When I have a new client, I always check for retained primitive and postural reflexes. Fear paralysis reflex (the first embryonic reflex) is detected not by doing a test but by checking with the mother about traumas in pregnancy or childbirth. One day, I was driving twenty-five miles to an orphanage to check for retained reflexes of a thirteen-year-old girl, Juana. You already know part of her story from Chapter 1. As I was in my car, I realized that I was faced, for the first time, with checking the retained reflexes of a child whose mother was not available to answer my questions.

It turned out that Juana had all but one reflex—headrighting—already inhibited, so I need not have worried. However, while testing her, I also tested the orphanage staff person who had asked me to check Juana. She giggled and moved through the palmar, plantar, and spinal Galant tests. In the end, it was the staff person who received a list of activities to complete in order to integrate her retained reflexes.

Sebastian

Another example of detecting the fear paralysis reflex took place later in the afternoon on the same day I tested Juana. While realizing my plight with the orphan girl, I never thought to be the least bit worried about testing a ten-year-old boy who came from a good home, with not only two parents, a brother, and a sister but also two sets of grandparents who adored him. Yet the test with Sebastian turned out just the opposite of what Juana had shown and what I had expected: Sebastian did not exhibit having integrated even one of the twelve reflexes.

I contacted his mother to ask her to talk with me about her son's birth and said, "It appears something traumatic happened during pregnancy or birth. None of his reflexes was integrated."

Sebastian's mother replied, "Traumatic? Yes, that would be the word. They almost lost me—and him! I was in labor for more than twenty-four hours. The doctors performed an emergency C-section. Sebastian was born purple and blue all over, with the cord wrapped around his neck."

Now, *that* birth experience is what indicates retained reflexes from birth.

Sebastian was a third-grader at the German School of Guatemala. He evidenced attention deficit hyperactivity disorder (ADHD) symptoms, which is often the case when the ATNR has not initiated. You can read more about Sebastian, his ADHD, and his curiosity in the chapter on ADD.

Sebastian was one of my hardest workers. He worked on his retained reflexes at home daily and with me once or twice a week. When one is working one-on-one with a child, one does not see the same ADHD behaviors that students display in the classroom. In Sebastian's case, he was a willing learner and did his daily exercises like clockwork.

When I saw him at his school, he would immediately start cross-crawling and tell me, "Yes, I did my exercises before school this morning."

Sebastian made progress in all areas in which we worked. He had not integrated any of his primitive or postural reflexes before he came to Brain Ways, yet he integrated all of his retained reflexes within four months. His left-right-left-right exercises helped lower his distractibility in the classroom. He passed all his classes. Together, we completed Structure of Intellect (SOI) modules, homework, English grammar, The Listening Program (TLP), the Belgau Platform Balance Board, and crossing-the-midline, brain-bag activities. (You will learn more about these in following chapters.)

Sebastian represented his school in Destination Imagination and made it to the finals in the United States a couple of years later. The mission of Destination Imagination is to "develop opportunities that inspire the global community of learners to utilize diverse approaches in applying [twenty-first-century] skills and creativity" (www.destinationimagination.org). I would like to think the work we did for over a year helped prepare him for that contest. As this book is heading to print, Sebastian has recently graduated high school.

Jacob

Jacob, age five, also tested with all twelve reflexes retained. However, when I asked his mother about his birth, she said it was "a piece of cake, no problems." I was stumped for only a second, as I then asked about her pregnancy.

Jacob was in the womb and in the midst of a very critical developmental stage when 9/11 happened. His mother and father were on a business trip to China when the Twin Towers fell in New York. His mother believed that planes would never fly again and that she would never be able to return home to her two-year-old, to her family, to her life. I believe this worry continued for two weeks before the couple felt safe enough to fly home. While living with his mom's fears in utero, Jacob obviously missed some of his developmental inhibiting of reflexes. Subsequently, the following reflexes could not inhibit either. It took more than a year for him to integrate all twelve retained reflexes. Mostly, he worked with me in the office, rather than doing his exercises alone at home.

ACTION GUIDE: EXERCISES TO INTEGRATE RETAINED REFLEXES

What needs to be accomplished to integrate any of the twelve primitive and postural reflexes that a client retains? Lack of use is one of the reasons they persist. One thing to do is to bring on the reflex and repeat it until it fatigues. If a reflex did not inhibit in the womb or before age two—or, for that matter, on its own in childhood or adulthood—then exercises and activities can also be performed to help integrate each reflex. As I mentioned, Sebastian was totally integrated after performing exercises for just four months. The exercises that work for children also work on adults in the same way.

1. Fear Paralysis Reflex
(and All the Succeeding Retained Reflexes)
The Infinity Sign, Lying-on-Its-Side Lazy 8, or Active 8: Center the infinity sign on the wall in front of you. Follow the ∞ around with your right hand, left hand, or both. Keep looking at your moving hand(s) with your eyes. *Brain Gym: Teacher's Edition* reads: "As the eyes follow the flowing movement of the hands, they learn to focus together for binocular case" (Dennison and Dennison 2010, 32). The body stays in the middle of the 8, where the lines cross, but the eyes should follow the movement

of the hand(s) through space, on the lines of the Active 8. This action is helpful in integrating retained reflexes (O'Hara 2003b).

You can also engage your core by working on a balance board while completing the 8s. Look out over the outstretched arm pointing at the 8. This helps with integration of auditory and visual skills. For improvement in handwriting, the 8s can be done large, with your shoulder trying to touch your ear and your eyes looking up [to the] right, using the right hand, or up [to the] left with your left hand (Dennison and Dennison, 1987, 40).

Fear Paralysis and All Subsequent Reflexes (Heart 8, Shirshasana 8, and Solar Plexus 8): Each of these 8s entails making an Active 8 with your hand in front of a different part of your body: in front of the heart (Heart 8); above the head (Shirshasana 8), on both the horizontal and the vertical plane; and in front of the lower ribs and stomach area (the Solar Plexus 8). All three help to integrate retained reflexes (O'Hara 2004, 11).

In another helpful exercise, the child lies on his back with brain bags placed on his cheeks and jaws and then holds more bags to his ears. Another person holds the Positive Points—above the person's eyebrows, centered above the pupils of the eyes—for one to two minutes while the child does belly breathing very slowly (O'Hara 2004, 52).

2. MORO REFLEX

A game I always play, which the children love, is called the Eagle and the Rabbit. (I play it a bit differently than Brendan taught it.) As I share the story of the eagle, I "fly" around the child, who is lying on his back. A brain bag is on his stomach, representing food. The eagle, who is searching for his breakfast, swoops down and tries to grab the bag. At the same time, the child grabs the bag and hides it within his grasp in fetal position, bringing his legs in and hugging his knees. The eagle "flies" away without breakfast, so the rabbit stretches out again. Little kids especially like "winning" over the eagle, and they perform many of the necessary in-and-out movements while doing so (2004, 49).

Heart 8s: Inscribe an infinity sign in the air, with the heart chakra as the central crossover point. Always begin in the middle, going up and out, and swap the beanbag from one hand to the other at the center. (Song: "Up and around and down and in. Swap hands swap hands," *Beanbag Ditties* CD, copyright O'Hara 2014.)

drawing © Brendan O'Hara, 2014

Hey Um: Hold the beanbag in your right hand. Reach out and up with both hands, up on your toes. At the top, swap the beanbag to your left hand. Then bring your arms out and down, squat down, and swap hands at the bottom. The beanbag will inscribe a circle/oval as you pass it from hand to hand. Repeat several times. (Song: "Hey Um Whey Um," *Beanbag Ditties* CD, copyright O'Hara 2014.)

drawing © Brendan O'Hara, 2014

Slide: Sitting with legs out in front and leaning back on hands, place a beanbag on your left knee. Slide your left hand along your outer thigh and pick up the beanbag, placing it on your right knee as you raise it. Put your hands and knee down. Repeat on the other side. Do many cycles. (Song: "Slide. Pick it up. Put it on the other knee, Hands back," *Beanbag Ditties* CD, copyright O'Hara 2014.)

drawing © Brendan O'Hara, 2014

Starfish: If your child is in vision therapy at an optometrist's office, they will probably practice the Starfish in attempting to integrate the Moro reflex. The child is sitting up straight, crossing their leg over the other leg, and making a fist with their hand over the other hand, as the drawing indicates. Then the child leans back over the pillow while stretching out their hands, arms, and legs again. Hold this outstretched starfish-looking pose for six to eight seconds, and repeat twice more, sitting up, interchanging which foot/leg and arm/hand is in front of the other, leaning back, opening like a starfish, and breathing deeply.

drawing by Teryn Brown

3. PALMAR REFLEX

The way to suppress this reflex is to continue to do as we did in the assessment: stroke the hand from the outer edges to the center many times. Do this until the reflex is suppressed. It can also be integrated by squeezing a tennis ball many times. A variation with the tennis ball is to squeeze each finger sequentially back and forth.

Head Drop, Orange Drop, We Move Our Hands Through the Air, and Beat the Drum are integrating activities for the palmar reflex, also found on the CD that accompanies the book *Movement and Learning Beanbag Ditties* (copyright O'Hara 2014).

4. INFANT PLANTAR & BABINSKI REFLEXES

Marbles: The typical way to integrate this reflex is to have a child pick up marbles or crayons with their toes. You can also use a pointer or paintbrush to mimic the test by stroking the sole of the foot a number of times, a few times a day. Eventually, as the plantar reflex integrates, there will be no reaction by the child. Some brain bag activities that help integrate the plantar reflex are Ankle 8s, Beanbag Pickup, Dead Drop to Feet, One-Legged Humming Game, and Cone Spiral (O'Hara 2004, 17).

5. TONIC LABYRINTHINE REFLEX

TLR 8s entail standing while doing the 8s. Holding the brain bag at the navel, start the infinity sign simultaneously with the left hand and left foot. The learner completes the Active 8 by moving the other foot out and to the side and back while moving the brain bag in the other hand around and back to the navel. Complete nine to ten cycles (O'Hara 2004, 88).

Crawling and creeping fulfill both training and inhibitory process. According to Goddard, page 19: "Both facilitate integration of sensory information as vestibular, visual, and proprioceptive systems all start to operate together for the first time."

If you are taking Vision Therapy at a qualified optometrist office that offers VT, you might be able to do the bridge and snow angels to not only integrate the TLR, but also improve visual skills:

The Bridge entails lifting the body with the feet as close to the body as possible and breathing in deeply for a count of ten, relaxing and repeating three sets.

Snow Angels are relatively complicated as your child will need to lie down on the floor and move their upper limbs to reach the top at the exact same time the legs reach their maximum "openness width." Then from position of hands touching above head on the floor, the child has to move her arms down and touch the side of the body at the exact time the spread-out legs close to touch each other. It helps to count to ten aloud while trying to time the arms and legs to touch at the same time.

*exercise performed on the floor

Head Drop: Place a beanbag on top of your head. Tilt head forward (chin down) so that the beanbag drops. As it falls, catch the beanbag below your navel. Drop the beanbag to the back by tilting your head backward (chin up) and catching it behind the back, level with the sacrum. You could drop the beanbag into a basket or simply let it drop onto the floor (copyright Brendan O'Hara, 2014).

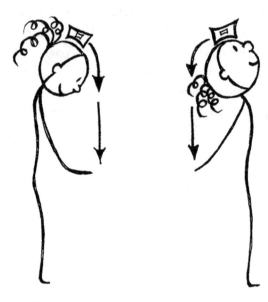

drawing © Brendan O'Hara, 2014

Rib Cage Breathing: Hug yourself, and squeeze the air out of your lungs. Breathe in against the pressure of your hug. Force your rib cage to expand. Keep your shoulders down and your stomach passive. To add to the effectiveness, you can put a beanbag on your head (copyright Brendan O'Hara, 2014).

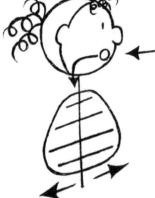

drawing © Brendan O'Hara, 2014

6. ASYMMETRICAL TONIC NECK REFLEX

I have children crawl across my office rugs while holding a brain bag or a hacky sack between their head and shoulder, with their head turned to one side. At the end of the rugs, they turn around to come back, switch the bag or sack to the other shoulder, and turn their head the other way. Repeat four to five times with each head turn.

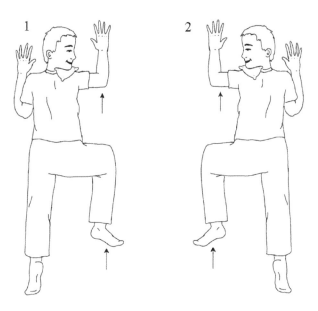

ATNR Eyes: While the child is standing, the left hand takes the brain bag out to the left side at shoulder level. The head turns to follow the bag. The left hand returns to the midline and gives the bag to the right hand at the sternum. The eyes follow, with the head turned at shoulder level and out to the right. The bag returns to the sternum and switches to the left hand. Repeat this cycle, turning the head fifteen to twenty times. Repeat the same actions, except, in this cycle of ten to fifteen repetitions, turn the head in the direction *opposite* the brain bag. The eyes focus on the bag only as it is being swapped from one hand to the other (O'Hara 2004, 37–8).

ATNR Eyes with Knees: Raise the opposite knee of the hand holding the brain bag (O'Hara 2004, 37–8).

Round and Round My Tummy: The beanbag circles the body below the navel (swapping from one hand to the other in front and behind). Circle both ways; always finish in a clockwise direction. (Song: "Beanbag, beanbag. Beanbag goes around. Round and round my tummy. Round and round my tummy. Beanbag, beanbag," *Beanbag Ditties* CD, copyright Brendan O'Hara 2014.)

drawing © Brendan O'Hara, 2014

Waves: Both hands commence at your navel. One hand takes the beanbag on a journey. It travels down and out, up and around to above the head, and straight down the midline to give it to the other hand, which is waiting at the navel. Repeat the same movement on the other side. Do many cycles. (Song: "The waves come in. The waves go out all around and all about." *Beanbag Ditties* CD, copyright Brendan O'Hara, 2014.)

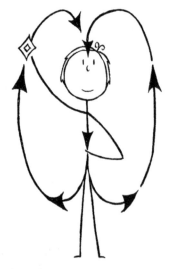

drawing © Brendan O'Hara, 2014

7. SPINAL GALANT REFLEX

Quiet Tiger, Arching Cat, and Resting Tiger: In cat position, with bags on top of head, quiet tigers rock forward and backward and sway sideways. Children can vocalize a tiger's roar (quietly). Do this with your eyes open, closed, and blinking. Add brain bags on your hands, feet, back, and hips. Lift the bags on and off. Apply pressure to sides of the shoulders and hips. Drop bags on. Arching cat is like cat pose in yoga: Inhale while raising the head and lowering the stomach, so the back becomes concave. Exhale while lowering head and stretching the spine upward, and contract abdomen. Bags should be on your back. Start the movements from the sacrum. Resting Tiger follows Arching Cat. Bags should be on your back. Take a few breaths with your hands and forehead resting on the rug, as in yoga's child's pose. Sit back on your feet. Feel your sacrum moving with your breath (O'Hara 2004, 73–7).

8. SUCKING AND ROOTING REFLEX

The best way to inhibit this reflex is to repeat the test many times until the reflex is no longer present. Take a pointer, pencil, or paintbrush and slowly stroke from the cheek toward the corners of the lips. Repeat this movement, starting in the middle of the chin and proceeding toward the edges of the lips. As I mentioned, it is quite difficult to see each little twitch or smile, so this is a foolproof way to integrate. Keep repeating.

ESR Supine: Lie down on a rug, holding a brain bag on your mouth (place a tissue between your mouth and the bag), cheeks, and chin. Someone holds the positive points on the face about one inch higher than the pupils on the forehead (O'Hara 2004, 25, 52).

9. SYMMETRICAL TONIC NECK REFLEX

In cat position, as with the reflexes test, the child drops his head as if he is looking at his belly button and holds for a count of five. Then, trying to move only his head, the child lifts his head and looks at the ceiling. Repeat five times daily until the extra movement of the body stops and the reflex is integrated.

10. VESTIBULAR REFLEX

Pineal 8s: In the reflexes workshop, there are also a number of Active 8s designed specifically to integrate the vestibular. One is called Pineal 8s. "The pineal chakra is the center of flowing movement" (O'Hara 2004,72).

It is performed in front of the forehead because the pineal gland is located in the brain behind the forehead.

Tall 8s: Another vestibular exercise, Tall 8s, uses the whole body. These are done together on the same vertical plane, moving a brain bag around the feet, up past the chest, and above the head. "Starting at the navel, right hand takes beanbag up and around to above head, as body stretches up onto toes. Beanbag is passed to left hand above the head. Left hand carries beanbag out, down, and in to meet and give it to the right hand at the navel. Right hand then carries beanbag down and around to meet left hand at floor level. Left hand carries it up again to the navel. Squat down so beanbag reaches close to the floor. Do many rounds. Slow and smooth. Hum a note that makes you feel good" (2004, 84).

- **Humming Game:** "The One-Legged Humming Game is another game for balance and improved 'proprioception,' the term used to describe the communication between the brain and the muscles. In a circle (or individually) everyone hums whilst standing on one leg, bobbing slowly up and down (i.e. bending the knee): First one leg and then the other. It can be more complex:

- Patting the head with one hand
- Patting the tummy with one hand
- Patting head & tummy simultaneously
- Head turning
- Eyes closed, etc. Let your creativity lead you." (O'Hara 1991a, 2016, 28)

Other Exercises: Walking on a walking rail, which people can make at home with wood from a lumberyard, and jumping on the trampoline are also easy ways to challenge the vestibular.

11. HEADRIGHTING REFLEX

One basic exercise can be used if the headrighting reflex is retained: I ask clients to perform the same movement of the head and shoulders, as in the assessment, again and again. However, this time I place a (rice-filled) brain bag on top of the head so the person is aware and makes sure it doesn't fall off. This ensures that the head stays upright during practice.

12. AMPHIBIAN REFLEX

One basic exercise can be used if the amphibian reflex is retained. Clients need to learn to crawl the correct way. Move the left leg and right arm and hand forward at the same time, followed by the right leg and left arm and hand. Practice to integrate this reflex. (Note: the feet should drag behind the legs, not be upright or off the ground.) Once the child can crawl correctly, the reflex will integrate over time.

CHAPTER 3:

Eyesight, Vision, and Visual Skills

DO YOU KNOW THE DIFFERENCE between "eyesight" and "vision"? Initially, I didn't. But what a difference there is! "Eyesight" is the ability to see small things—acuity. It is the function of the eyeball. The lens, cornea, and retina determine acuity. "Vision," however, surpasses the function of the eyeball. The brain is interpreting that which is being seen. The brain is where vision happens.

If a person is unconscious, one can produce an image on the retina (eyesight), but the person cannot tell you what s/he is seeing (vision).

Vision requires the brain to interpret what the retina "sees," and then respond accordingly.

If a person has acuity, good eyesight, then, on the Snellen Eye Chart test—the chart that is used in doctors' offices, the Department of Motor Vehicles, and schools—there will be a good, crisp image in the retina. (If a person is vision-"able," s/he has visual skills. S/he has the ability to refocus his or her eyes for convergence, divergence, teaming, binocularity, or flexibility.) Eye muscles acting together require the brain to interpret what the retina sees. The retina sees, and the brain responds.

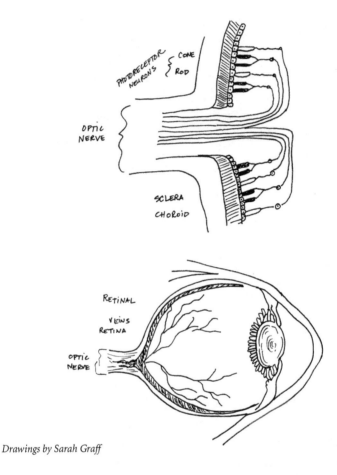

Drawings by Sarah Graff

It is so rewarding to complete vision therapy (VT) with children and adults because vision problems can often be corrected in a finite length of time or a finite number of VT sessions.

In my practice, post-classroom work, I have informed parents with this statement: "I believe your child's vision is the problem."

The typical response is, "Oh, it can't be. S/he just had an eye exam and has 20/20 vision." Those 20/20 numbers tell me that we are talking about eyesight, not vision.

How do people acquire "good" or "bad" vision? Are people born with their own type of vision? And how is VT used to improve visual skills?

Vision is a learned skill. As a baby's reflexes begin to inhibit or integrate, his/her vision skills begin to develop. As a baby moves through his/her many developmental stages, vision continues to develop. If a baby or young child misses an important developmental milestone, his/her visual skills will not develop appropriately. For instance, a baby who has a traumatic pregnancy or birth will more than likely have vision problems because the developmental stages of acquiring primitive and postural reflexes are built one after another.

New parents are now learning about ways to improve their child's eyesight and vision in the early months. High-contrast colors, or black and white, are optimum for young babies' visual development. There are now many baby brands that offer nearly everything a baby could use in striking black-and-white stripes or designs. There is also an increasing number of books for babies in high-contrast black and white, including *Look Look* by Peter Linenthal, and *Black on White* and *Black & White* by Tana Hoban.

As a baby nurses, the mother naturally changes from one breast to another. A mother cannot just nurse from one breast because the other breast is also full of milk. As a baby is attached, one eye is nestled in with the mother while the other eye is able to build muscles and vision moving all around. Then, when the mother switches the baby to the other breast, the other eye gets its chance to develop. Problems happen, I believe, when breastfeeding is replaced by a bottle. If both parents, two sets of grand-parents, and most babysitters are right-handed, they tend to hold the baby in their left arm and hold the baby bottle in their right. When does the baby's right eye get a chance to exercise? Nearly never.

So, children who don't have two "equal" eyes are handicapped from the get go. And even if the two eyes have exercised and developed, they still need to expose the brain to "teaming" or working together binocu-larly. Children need to crawl to do this; standing right up and walking will not develop binocularity. Children who do not crawl, or who crawl for less than one month, need other activities to develop binocular abilities with their eyes/brain. Otherwise, when it is time to read and each eye must focus on a word in the same place at the same time, it just will not happen.

In crawling, the baby's eyes are practicing looking out in front of him/her in the distance and up close. The muscles that began develop-ing independently are now learning to synchronize, to "team," to work together. There are neural pathways developing in the brain as the child crawls heterolaterally, with the left leg and right arm/hand moving at the same time, followed by the right leg with left arm/hand movement. Dendrites are forming, linking the left and right hemispheres. Children who miss crawling need other activities to stimulate the development of binocular focus.

Kindergarten used to be a developmental time for gross- and fine-motor skills. In countries like the United States, however, kindergarten has turned into a mini–test prep center where parents are worried about their child reading "early" and getting into the best university. Hence, developmental motor skills receive little or no time in the curriculum.

I am working with a family in VT at the time of this writing. The eleven-year-old son cannot track, which means that he does not move his eyes from the beginning of each line to the end, with a return to the beginning of the next line. This is making it hard for him to read. The mother finally under-stands the importance of crawling, but she did not know this ten years ago.

"If parents would only get down on their knees and move their child in the proper left-right-left-right sequence on hands and knees," I told her, "vision therapists would have fewer clients."

She agreed, saying, "I would have done so, if only I had known."

That is the problem.

Parents and grandparents watch their baby crawling, using his/her backside, pushing with one hand and one leg on the same side, and think, "Isn't it cute how differently s/he crawls?"

But the baby needs to look with the two eyes level into the midline visual field while the legs/arms move cross-laterally to develop their brain's visual skills.

Further development of the visual system in the brain is augmented or accelerated by outdoor play. Big-muscle movement and gross-motor skills develop neural pathways related to vision in the brain. In pioneer days, children were outside working. Similar activities took place with children in farming communities. Then, post–World War II, with the advent of tract housing, outdoor play with neighbor kids was the norm for baby boomers. Today's children, in contrast, spend much less time outside. Many parents do take their babies, toddlers, and preschoolers to Gymboree and other exercise classes, but I am not sure how much these aid in eye-muscle development and eye "teaming," especially considering that classes take place only one or two times per week.

The increase in the need for VT, in my opinion, is directly related to the proliferation of video games, especially handheld Nintendos and the like. A child who sits and plays video games for hours is not outside exercising gross-motor skills (which, in turn, enhances fine-motor skill development). The vestibular and eye muscles are not being challenged, so the brain is not strengthening binocularity or any of the other visual skills that need to be learned in childhood. The handheld device/video-game craze has probably decelerated the development of the visual system in many children. When I look at the ten- to fourteen-year-old range with whom I have worked on vision skills, specifically the boys, there are few who are not avid PlayStation players!

While writing about gross- and fine-motor skills, I want to mention interrelated visual-perceptual skills, which also should be developing as a child grows and interacts with his/her environment. Basic perceptual skills are absolutely necessary for a child to succeed in reading. Poor visual motor skills are usually caused by immature, underdeveloped gross-motor and balance (vestibular) skills. It is extremely important that a child who has immature perceptual motor skills be identified and given help early.

For many years when I taught kindergarten, we had activities and worksheets to develop the visual-perceptual skills of the students. As the years went on, the emphasis in kindergarten shifted to reading and writing, without taking into account these underlying skills. They are extremely important for reading. In the action guide at the end of this chapter are lists of games, books, and activities to help develop visual-perceptual skills. In VT, these are the visual-perceptual skills we test and work with:

- Visual discrimination
- Visual memory
- Visual-spatial relationships
- Visual form constancy
- Visual sequential memory
- Visual figure-ground
- Visual closure

VERGENCE INSUFFICIENCY

Convergence insufficiency is the most common visual skill deficiency. "Convergence" is the movement of the eyes turning inward or toward each other. Difficulty with that coordinated movement is called "convergence insufficiency." When we are not able to converge our eyes easily and accurately, these problems may develop:

- Eye strain
- Headaches
- Double vision
- Difficulty reading and concentrating
- Avoidance of near work
- Poor sports performance
- Dizziness or motion sickness

Generally, children think that everyone sees the world as they do. Thus, for example, a child may experience double vision (diplopia) but may not be aware that this is not normal. Indeed, it is quite common for children who are struggling with reading and other close work—especially in school—to experience seeing double after a relatively short amount of reading. These children will often simply avoid reading or say that they don't like to read.

In such cases, the children are usually experiencing difficulties with eye coordination and eye strain at close distances. A doctor from the College of Optometrists in Vision Development (COVD) is qualified to determine the cause of and make any necessary referrals for the treatment of diplopia and any other convergence, divergence, and visual skills deficiencies. Two tools for identification are the Convergence Insufficiency Symptom Survey (CISS) (see the Action Guide at the end of this chapter) and a parent survey like the one used at Larkspur Landing Optometry. Of course, an eye exam by a developmental optometrist is necessary to follow up on these questionnaires and to diagnose the visual skills.

If a parent has more than two "yes" answers in the questionnaire printed in this chapter, it is an indication that the child might benefit from an eye exam with the COVD optometrist and possibly from VT.

Welcome to Larkspur Landing Optometry!   Date_____

Pediatric Vision Questionnaire

Child's Name_____   Birthdate____/____/_____

School _____ Teacher_____ Grade _____

Referred to this office by _____

Why do you feel your child needs a vision exam? _____

Date of last vision exam _____ Doctor's name_____

Were glasses prescribed? _____ Family history of vision problems? _____

Has vision therapy or patching been recommended?_____

School performance up to potential?_____

Frowns or squints to see something? _____

Complains of print "running together" or "moving around?" _____

Gets tired or has headaches after reading or studying? _____

One eye turns in or out? If so, when? _____

Red eyes or eyelids? _____

Eyes water? Or, rubs eyes frequently? _____

Closes or covers one eye? When? _____

Skips or rereads words or letters? _____

Uses finger as marker when reading?_____

Reverses letters when writing (b for d, p for q)? _____

Poor recall of visually presented materials? _____

Difficulty with spelling? _____

Transposition of letters or numbers ((21 for 12)? _____

Makes errors in copying from whiteboard to paper? _____

Poor handwriting? _____

Clumsiness? _____

Child currently working with learning specialists (speech, OT)? _____

Eye coordination problems like convergence insufficiency generally cannot be improved with eyeglasses or surgery. A program of VT is needed to improve eye coordination abilities and reduce symptoms and discomfort when doing close work.

It is necessary for both eyes to work together, especially in tasks such as reading. In VT, the Brock string—a long string with three colored beads named after Dr. Frederick W. Brock, who developed the string to train his own eyes, and can be used to correct both convergence and divergence—is my favorite way to train convergence. There is a great YouTube video (FantasticElasticBrain.com/videos) that shows what the eyes are supposed to see when looking at a Brock string. I urge you to take a look. It clearly shows how the eyes "see" the two lines. Using the Harmon Distance, which is a measure from the middle finger's middle knuckle to the elbow, to mimic the distance from the eyes to a book while reading, I place one bead on a string, setting the bead at exactly the Harmon Distance measured. Then, I ask the client to focus on that bead and answer this question: "The two lines coming out of your face and the two lines coming out of my face form an X." (I also hold one string on my nose with the bead between us.) "Do the lines cross on the bead, before the bead, or after the bead?"

When I have the answer, I can tell if the client has sufficient convergence, is under convergent, or is over convergent. If the X crosses on the ball, then the person is able to converge both his/her eyes on the same words when reading. If the lines appear to cross before the bead, we can assume the eyes are over convergent. If the lines appear to cross after the bead, we assume the eyes are under convergent. It is useful to know, as well, if there is suppression on one side or the other, which is indicated if the person says the string "goes in and out" or "disappears at times."

I had a fun experience with a client, Cecilia, who had tested very under convergent with the Brock string. I wanted her to know, to experience, what it was like to have the two strings cross on the bead. Then she would experience the convergence I wanted her to develop by doing Brock string exercises. My friend Mary Alice held the string out in front of Ceci with one bead at the Harmon Distance. Ceci was standing on the Belgau Platform Balance Board, holding the string on her nose. I then pushed her shoulders while she resisted, trying to get her body to the exact point where she would see the X cross on the bead.

As she was resisting, she said, "Yes, now I see the strings cross on the bead!"

The funny part came about ten minutes later, when her mother came to pick her up. Ceci explained, "Hey, Mom. All I have to do is hold books over here," and she twisted her body and held an imaginary book out to her right, "and then I can read just perfectly!"

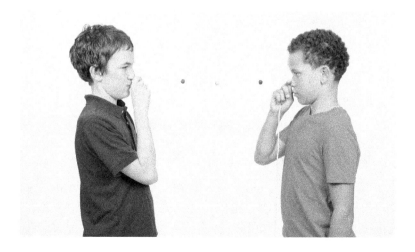

What can teachers do to assist students with convergence insufficiency? I do not know if Dr. Brock, with his invention of the Brock string, ever thought it would be a mainstay of every classroom in the world, but I think it should be. If a child has optimum convergence, it will not bother the child to practice what is already a learned skill. For the child whose convergence is insufficient, practicing moving his/her focus from one bead to the other and back again is giving the brain time to adjust, to focus, to converge or diverge, and then move on. The muscles exercise and the brain "learns" as the focus moves from one bead to another. If every child in the world had a Brock string, and every teacher allowed kids to exercise with it twice a day, many convergence insufficiencies could be improved.

Obviously, an exam by a COVD optometrist and ensuing VT would be ideal. However, access to convergence exercises at school could assist those children without access to VT. The eyes watering or feeling "funny" or sore is a quick indicator that the person or the child's parent should locate a behavioral optometrist. You can locate a COVD behavioral optometrist at www.covd.org.

When individuals engage in VT, they often use Polaroid lenses to work with vectograms. Convergence, divergence, accommodation, eye-hand coordination, and other visual skills can be improved with vectogram work. This is not an activity for home; one uses vectograms in VT.

There are various exercises using vectograms that help the person improve his/her visual skills. A YouTube video (FantasticElasticBrain. com/videos) shows a short piece on vectograms. If a child needs VT, s/he will undoubtedly work on skills using vectograms.

There is another little contraption, called an "aperture rule," that can be used. One looks through a small rectangle at two objects on a card that are spaced apart. As one moves the tiny rectangle farther away from the objects-picture, there is a greater need to converge the two eyes in order to see the tiny + and • in the merge or fusion of the two pictures, as they are spaced farther and farther apart. Hence the eyes and brain "practice" the convergence that is needed for normal day-to-day activities such as reading or examining things close up. Alternatively, one can practice divergence using two openings in the aperture rule.

VISION PROBLEMS RESULTING FROM BRAIN INJURY

Head injuries impact people from all walks of life. Acquired brain injury (ABI) is an all-inclusive category for a variety of injuries that involve the brain. These can occur as a result of sports/recreational injuries, combat injuries, auto accidents, electrical shock, strokes, falls, or disease. Traumatic brain injury is a subset of ABI.

Regardless of the reason for the head injury, vision problems often occur as a result. They can be as severe as total vision loss or even partial loss. They can also be as subtle as an eye-coordination problem, which results in double vision, balance and movement problems, dizziness, and motion sickness.

There are a variety of different signs that one has a vision problem as a result of the head injury called Post Trauma Vision Syndrome (PTVS). PTVS was first described by William V. Padula, OD, the founding president of the Neuro Optometric Rehabilitation Association.

The good news is that most of the vision problems associated with PTVS are treatable with special lenses, prisms, or in-office optometric VT (www.covd.org).

POST-TRAUMA VISION SYNDROME CHECKLIST/ TRAUMATIC BRAIN INJURY

If you have had a head injury and now have any of the following symptoms, it is possible that you have a vision problem. Locate a doctor near you for a comprehensive evaluation. Some signs that you have a vision problem might include:

- Headaches
- Nausea
- Light sensitivity
- Staring behavior (low blink rate)
- Inability to keep your place when reading
- Spatial disorientation
- Difficulty shifting focus from near to far
- Associated neuromotor difficulties with balance, coordination, and posture
- Bumping into objects when walking (Gates 2012)

CLIENT SUCCESS

Jose Miguel

Jose Miguel completed the Structure of Intellect (SOI) assessment with me in Guatemala because I told his mother that I could tell her what was wrong—that I could explain why, for the past five years, his teachers had frequently told her there was something wrong with her son but never told her what the cause of his difficulty was. Or, worse, teachers would blame his difficulties on dyslexia, a diagnosis with which I did not agree. Jose Miguel also possessed some ADHD-like behaviors, such as looking away and seeming not to pay attention. He often showed distractibility and did not complete his work. Many children labeled ADHD or ADD actually lack visual skills.

Jose Miguel's SOI results showed that he scored low in a number of areas that could be related to vision. I was not able to find an available VT in Guatemala. The only doctor who offered a type of skills assessment at that time had a practice in which the patients would sometimes have to wait seven or eight hours to be seen.

Jose Miguel's parents were beyond thrilled to finally have an answer to their son's deficits in reading, specifically, and behaviors in school, generally. Jose Miguel's mother made flight reservations to Fort Lauderdale, Florida. Then, she spent her day on the Internet, researching and finding behavioral or developmental optometrists in the Fort Lauderdale area. She exchanged e-mails with a number of these doctors and finally made an appointment with Dr. M. in Westin, Florida.

On the Friday office examination, Dr. M. said he was not sure where Guatemala was or what a *gringa* was, but the woman who told her that her son had weak visual skills was correct. The examinations confirmed that indeed her son scored very low in most of the visual skills assessed.

Jose Miguel attended VT daily for two months in Dr. M.'s Florida clinic. When he had improved to the 80 percent level, he returned home to Guatemala, where he continued to perform VT exercises at home. When Jose Miguel returned to Florida a year later for a progress check, his visual skills were assessed at 90 percent. This improvement impacted his schoolwork, as his grades improved significantly.

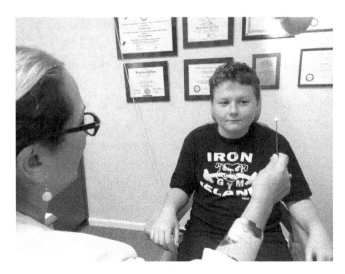

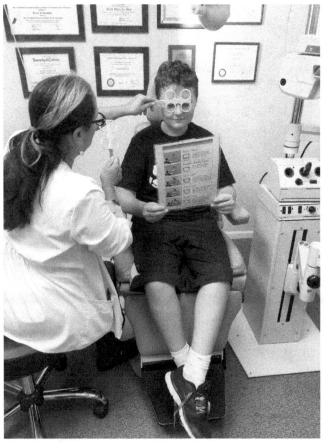

Thomas

When Thomas began VT in Larkspur, California, his mother marked a number of behaviors on the optometrist's checklist like the one in this chapter that indicated probable visual skills deficiencies. These included the following:

- His school performance was not up to potential.
- He had headaches after reading.
- He reversed or transposed letters and numbers such as b and d, p and q, and 12 and 21.
- Thomas had poor recall of visually presented materials.

After the doctor's examination, Thomas started VT in the optometrist's office with me.

Thomas's mother had purchased an Integrated Listening Systems (iLs) player for Thomas, but he had not used it or heard the music because he did not like the feel of the headphones on his ears. I asked Thomas if he would listen each time he visited my office for our VT sessions, and he agreed. He began to listen to the sensory motor playlist during our sessions and three other times during the week. I firmly believe it greatly assisted his rapid visual skills development.

The two most impressive improvements that Thomas's mother noted were made between September 2012 and March 2013, when Thomas's reading speed improved from 67 words per minute to 102. Also, his mother told me that for the previous two baseball seasons, Thomas had rarely hit the ball, but now this season, in the spring of 2013, he was making contact at bat in nearly every game, getting hits and scoring runs for his team. His developmental eye movement (DEM) test showed improvement. His written reversals were diminished in the Gardner test, which tests for reversals in reading and writing. He graduated from VT as a success!

Ricardo

Ricardo was twelve years old when he arrived at Brain Ways in Guatemala. His mother came to my office bearing reports from first, third, fifth, and seventh grade with test results stating that Ricardo had dyslexia. Seventh grade was a challenge for Ricardo. He was especially slow in finishing his homework each day.

After three sessions of assessments, Ricardo still had not exhibited much in the way of dyslexic behaviors. I administered the SOI assessment to gain a better picture of the aptitudes in learning that Ricardo possessed. A red flag appeared when a number of visual indicator scores were amassed in the low range. It appeared that, even with the glasses that Ricardo wore, he could not detect small changes in figures.

The next step seemed obvious to me, but I knew being in Guatemala might be a detriment. I wanted Ricardo to be tested for eyesight *and* vision by a College of Optometrists in Vision Development (COVD) optometrist. Luckily, within weeks, Ricardo was planning to travel to Los Angeles to spend more than a month with his cousins.

By Ricardo's second week in Los Angeles, his aunt had located a COVD optometrist less than a mile from her home and acquired an appointment for Ricardo. Soon, his mother received an e-mail explaining the various areas of skills in which her son was weak. It was both confirming and surprising to learn about Ricardo's Van Orden Star.

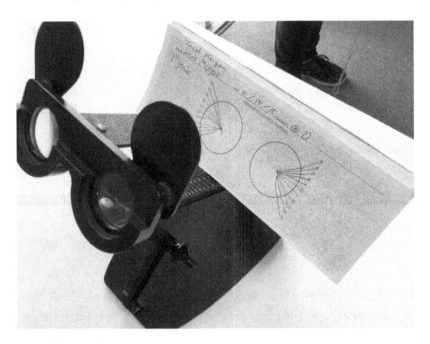

The Van Orden Star often shows suppression of vision on one side or the other; Ricardo showed suppression on both sides. In Ricardo's case, it showed that he literally saw things right in front of his face, whether they were close or not. I wondered how he managed to be such a good soccer player with this rather severe visual impediment. I also, once again, yearned for definitive data linking high use of video games and handheld Nintendos with visual skills deficiencies. I knew Ricardo fit that category, but I couldn't "prove" the connection with only one or two kids.

I knew that VT would improve Ricardo's visual skills, as well as his behavior issues and problems with schoolwork. I also knew that Ricardo could not spend an extra few months in Los Angeles, so I set about to learn as much as I could in order to help him. I paid close attention to the materials used and how the patients improved in accomplishing tasks as they progressed. I purchased books from Amazon and doctors' going-out-of-business items from eBay. There was even a Home Therapy System disc, which Ricardo used to improve his visual skills. I picked up ideas from YouTube from VT sites. I also visited two Los Angeles area doctors' VT clinics quite a number of times to view their VT sessions in action.

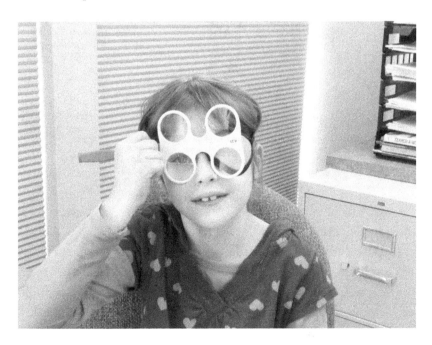

The doctor who had tested Ricardo helped me prepare to work with him. Many of the visual eye-hand coordination activities I had used in my years of teaching were in use at the VT sessions I observed and available for purchase: parquet pattern blocks, tangrams, geoboards, mazes, word searches, and visual-motor activities. Dr. Kenneth Lane's books, which included those items, linked a specific activity to a specific deficit, with ideas and activities to enhance or learn the missing skill. Eventually, I had enough new components to augment my usual Brain Ways work to improve Ricardo's visual skills.

In my Brain Ways practice, I was always challenging clients' vestibular reflex using Dr. Belgau's Platform Balance Board. In one office near Santa Barbara, I witnessed a number of clients receiving a small rebounder or trampoline from the doctor. The trampoline was an inexpensive and portable way for clients to challenge their vestibular while also working on improving visual skills. I became an advocate, especially as the doctor shared some of his photocopies of arrows for practicing and testing laterality. (The arrows pointed left, right, up, and down, which the kids had to track, say aloud, and show a directional movement for.) He also shared drawings of pigs and ducks. The children worked on their visual processing as they tracked the animals while jumping and making the appropriate sounds associated with the animal. I added trampoline exercises into my repertoire for Ricardo.

After working with Ricardo for some months, I wanted to be sure the vision work was improving him. We scheduled an appointment with Dr. Rosales, who noted that Ricardo's right eye would still wander off target when he tired. Ricardo needed more stamina work. We wanted both eyes to work together—to "team"—for long periods of time. Ricardo and I continued our work for a few more months, and then he continued with activities at home.

On his follow-up trip to Los Angeles the following October, Ricardo returned to the same optometrist and was retested. This time, his scores moved from "unskilled" and "marginal" to "skilled" in each area. His Van Orden Star finally resembled the star in the textbook.

He no longer saw everything, as ABC Sports TV used to say, "Up close and personal." Ricardo's worldview had literally and totally changed for the better. Since my first words, "It's a vision problem," Ricardo's parents had been hopeful that their son would no longer be diagnosed with dyslexia. As his visual skills improved during that year, his parents could see the "dyslexic-labeled problems" disappearing. Indeed, it was a label that had been put on Ricardo because he "saw" things differently. But now, with his new vision skills, he was no longer weak in binocularity, flexibility, tracking, saccades, pursuits, and other visual skills. Those "pesky problems," before labeled as dyslexia, disappeared.

Cecilia

Another young Guatemalan student, Cecilia, had been asked to leave her private school because she had not passed seventh grade. When I met her, she was once again in the process of failing seventh grade at another school. We began our Brain Ways assessments, including SOI testing. When I mentioned that we needed to work on her low visual skills, Ceci's dad wanted to know how she could have a vision problem when she could apply makeup like a professional. Nevertheless, her mother took her to the local eye doctor, who had studied in Colombia and knew about visual skills deficiencies. Ceci went to his clinic to work with the clinicians a number of times. Then, twice a week, I worked with her, repeating all of her vision exercises, accomplishing ones that were applicable in Dr. Lane's books, and completing her other Brain Ways work.

Ceci became my most accomplished student on the Belgau Platform Balance Board (see Chapter 5, "The Belgau Work"). We completed all of Dr. Belgau's lists of board activities, and then repeated them. While on the board, Ceci could knock off targets using her shoulders, wrists, or knees. She was incredible. And every move she made on the board with the Pendulum Ball was developing her two brain hemispheres as well as her visual skills.

As part of Ceci's VT, I also used a Visual Motor Control Stock (VMCS). The stick has colored bars, each one spaced equidistant from the center, so that a person hitting, for example, the yellow bar on the left can then hit the Pendulum Ball with the yellow on the right. Dr. Belgau also added numerals on the colored bars so, as a practitioner, I can say, "Hit the 6, then the 3" in order to have the learner hitting with his right side followed by his left side.

Sometimes Ceci would complain that using the VMCS was too hard. I would explain that I had practiced the same exercise that very day, and her competitive spirit would kick in. She would soon master the skill. Ceci's improvement in visual skills I believe was tied directly to that visual motor work with the control stick.

Although she didn't like working on the SOI modules (see Chapter 6, "Structure of Intellect"), Ceci had scored so low on many of the SOI attributes that I felt intensive work was necessary. She did very little in the way of homework, but when Ceci was in my office, she put forth the maximum effort and completed various SOI modules. She also improved her visual skills doing the close work of the SOI discrimination pages. She also listened to all ten of The Listening Program (TLP) discs during her twice-a-week sessions in my office.

After terminating the second year of seventh grade, Cecilia switched schools again. Within the first few months, she was #1 in her class. I think her abilities in the new school were a direct result of our having improved the visual skills that had been deficient.

ACTION GUIDE

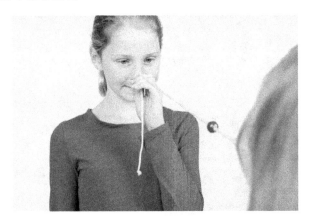

The first action you want to take is to complete the survey on the next page. Go through each question carefully and mark the appropriate answer as you read the prompts for your child.

Now add up the scores, using the point totals at the bottom of each column. If the score is 16 or more, it is likely that your child has convergence insufficiency.

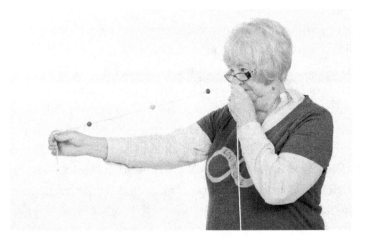

Convergence Insufficiency Symptom Survey

Name _____   DATE __/__/__

Clinician instructions: Read the following subject instructions and then each item exactly as written. If subject responds with "yes" - please qualify with frequency choices. **Do not give examples.**

Subject instructions: Please answer the following questions about how your eyes feel when reading or doing close work.

		Never	(not very often) Infrequently	Sometimes	Fairly often	Always
1.	Do your eyes feel tired when reading or doing close work?					
2.	Do your eyes feel uncomfortable when reading or doing close work?					
3.	Do you have headaches when reading or doing close work?					
4.	Do you feel sleepy when reading or doing close work?					
5.	Do you lose concentration when reading or doing close work?					
6.	Do you have trouble remembering what you have read?					
7.	Do you have double vision when reading or doing close work?					
8.	Do you see the words move, jump, swim or appear to float on the page when reading or doing close work?					
9.	Do you feel like you read slowly?					
10.	Do your eyes ever hurt when reading or doing close work?					
11.	Do your eyes ever feel sore when reading or doing close work?					
12.	Do you feel a "pulling" feeling around your eyes when reading or doing close work?					
13.	Do you notice the words blurring or coming in and out of focus when reading or doing close work?					
14.	Do you lose your place while reading or doing close work?					
15.	Do you have to re-read the same line of words when reading?					
		__ x 0	__ x 1	__ x 2	__ x 3	__ x 4

TOTAL SCORE _____

EXERCISES

Brock Strings: A Brock string—basically, a string with movable beads—can be made or purchased. An exercise, using the Brock string with three or more beads, can be completed daily to strengthen the eye muscles as well as the brain's view. Your child holds the string at different angles, with the beads set apart. Then your child focuses his/her eyes/brain on each bead until s/he sees an X at that bead made by the strings. Additionally, students can see the one in focus and use peripheral vision to "see" two each of the other beads. Both exercises strengthen the convergence and divergence abilities.

Pencil Push-ups: To work on eye-teaming skills, hold a pencil upright in front of your face. Slowly move the pencil toward your nose. Stop moving the pencil when you see two pencils. (It's best if you can have someone watching, in case one eye turns away.) Keep your eyes focused on the top of the pencil. Repeat a few times each day. The goal is to be able to move the pencil all the way to your nose without seeing double (two pencils).

Aperture Rule: The aperture-rule trainer can strengthen convergence and divergence skills. It is possible to purchase an aperture rule. It will help improve your eyes' ability to work together, so that you can do close work comfortably. The aperture rule consists of a long ruler set up on a stand on a rectangular platform. On one part of the ruler, there is a card holder. One uses the part with one rectangular opening for convergence training and the part with two rectangular openings for divergence training.

The reason I like the aperture rule is that the person doing the convergence or divergence work can see improvement easily when it happens. The cards' pictures spread farther and farther apart as the client moves from picture 1 through picture 12. I remember well the success that Ricardo felt after six months of being stuck on picture 1. The day came when he could progress through all the numeric positions.

The aperture rule that you purchase will come with directions. It is nearly impossible for me to explain the procedure without having an instrument with all its parts to demonstrate with, but there are YouTube videos that can give you a glimpse of an aperture rule, how to train with it, and the entire process (FantasticElasticBrain.com/videos).

Life Saver Card: Another exercise that is used in VT with follow-up at home is called the Life Saver card. There is a YouTube video that presents a step-by-step instruction (FantasticElasticBrain.com/videos) on the use of the transparent Life Saver card for work on divergence. To practice convergence, you use the opaque Life Saver card (FantasticElasticBrain. com/videos).

The same exercise can be used with any two objects drawn on a piece of paper at set apart from each other at different distances. I used to draw jack-o'-lanterns, clowns, and happy faces for my clients. On the left side, I would leave out certain facial characteristics like the eyes and nose. Then, on the right side, I would draw the same outline of the character but with only the missing facial characteristics.

I would have the client place a pencil tip between the two draw-ings and slowly move the pencil tip toward his/her nose while watching the tip. I would tell them to stop moving the pencil when the two objects were merged into one with the characteristics of both draw-ings. This exercise is for conver-gence. One would need to print the forms on a transparent sheet in order to practice for divergence as the pencil moves away from the drawings.

Walking Rail/Balance Beam (Balance, Vestibular): Construct your own with an eight-foot-long, 2x4 board held in place by three 4x4s nailed underneath. Have the child walk on the board with good posture and their head up in a heel-toe manner. They should walk backwards, forwards, and sideways. Place a brain bag on their head, and then have them pass it from hand to hand and toss/catch it. Next, place the brain bag in the middle of the rail and have the child pick it up, turn around, and put it back. My kids especially like to try to walk by as I swing the Pendulum Ball perpendicular to the rail.

Flashlight Game (Visual Motor): In a dim room, you and your child will each have a flashlight. Call out names of objects in the room while your child has to hit the "on" button and shine the light on the object as quickly as possible. Also, have your child copy your light as you make shapes, letters, or numbers on the wall and s/he tells you what it is.

Visual-perceptual skills develop over time. The following activities can enhance those skills.

Play games such as:

- Spot It! (tracking, figure ground, visual discrimination)
- Pix Mix! (figure ground)
- Mental Blox (visualization)

- Hi, Ho, Cherry-O (eye-hand coordination, visual discrimination)
- Blink card game (visual form constancy)
- Bop It! (eye-hand coordination and memory skills)
- Memory game or with a regular deck of cards (visual-spatial relationships)
- I Spy Eagle Eye (figure ground, eye-hand coordination)

Read books and magazines such as:

- *I Spy* (figure-ground, visual discrimination)
- *Where's Waldo?* (figure-ground, visual discrimination)
- *Highlights* (the puzzles and Hocus Focus)

Do activities such as:

- Lite Brite (convergence, eye-hand coordination)
- Geoboards (visual spatial)
- Parquetry blocks (convergence, divergence, visual spatial)
- Parquet pattern blocks (ocular-motor)
- Tangrams (visualization)
- Mazes (tracking, saccades)
- Word searches (figure-ground, visual discrimination)
- Crawling and creeping heterolaterally (gross motor, fine motor, binocularity)

Another source I recommend is www.eyecanlearn.com. This site offers eye exercises for many visual skills. There are many sources for visual skill development: playing cards with your child, playing games, drawing, and coloring. I hope this chapter, with its success stories and Action Guide, encourages you.

CHAPTER 4:

Amblyopia, Strabismus, and Vision Therapy

THIS CHAPTER FOCUSES ON amblyopia (lazy eye) and strabismus (crossed eyes). Amblyopia is a condition in which one eye has poorer visual acuity than expected with prescription lenses. The "lazy eye" nickname is derived from the thought that the eye with clearer vision must do the bulk of the work of seeing, while the "lazy" eye just goes along for the ride, not doing much work at all.

Many people confuse lazy eye with strabismus, which can be crossed eyes or any type of eye turn. But lazy eye is a separate condition that can exist with or without strabismus. One or a variety of causes can be attributed to this difficulty. High amounts of nearsightedness, farsightedness, astigmatism, or the presence of a constant eye turn can cause the brain to suppress (turn off) the information in that eye. This suppression negatively impacts the development of clear vision.

According to COVD.org, the brain normally receives two images at slightly different angles, and it combines them to produce a 3-D image.

With amblyopia, the brain suppresses one of these images, which negatively impacts a person's binocular vision. S/he may have a number of functional vision problems, such as poor depth perception and poor eye tracking.

Likewise, strabismus impacts an individual's functional vision. Dr. Susan Barry, who has strabismus herself, explains in her book, *Fixing My Gaze*, what happens when binocular vision doesn't work correctly. Hers is an amazing story. Any reader of this book who has amblyopia or strabismus can be energized just by reading about this forty-seven-year-old woman using VT to finally see in 3-D.

In the last chapter, I wrote of the Brock string. In *Fixing My Gaze*, Barry explains how she used the Brock string so successfully in VT:

> When I learned to use the "Brock string," I received the feedback that I needed to know where my eyes were pointing and then to redirect them so that they were aiming simultaneously at the same point in space.

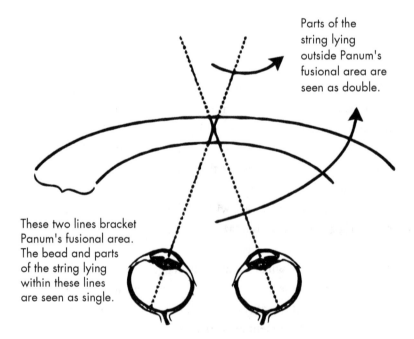

Parts of the string lying outside Panum's fusional area are seen as double.

These two lines bracket Panum's fusional area. The bead and parts of the string lying within these lines are seen as single.

Panum's fusional area. Each dotted line represents the line of sight for each eye.
© Margaret C. Nelson. Drawing from page 92 of Barry's book.

There is a small area right in front of and behind the fixation point where the images fall on almost corresponding retinal points. The area is called Panum's fusional area, and I could also fuse the images of those parts of the string that fell within this area. All other parts of the string fell outside Panum's fusional area and were seen as double. So, I saw four images of the string, two in front of and two behind the bead. This was fantastic feedback. Now I knew if I was suppressing input from one eye because then I would see only one image of the string in front of and behind the bead . . . With the Brock string, I could tell where in space my two eyes were looking! . . . I could turn in my eyes to point them at the closer bead and turn out my eyes to aim them at the more distant one, I knew that I had performed the procedure correctly if I could see the four string images emanating from the fixated bead. But above all, I could feel my eyes moving as a team! I could feel my eyes converge and diverge! (2010)

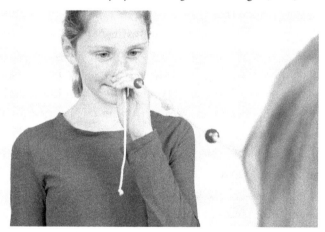

Dr. Barry adds, "I thought initially that this new-found skill applied only to the task at hand—but I was wrong" (2010). She then goes on to explain how the steering wheel in her car "popped out" at her. The next day, the rearview mirror popped out at her as well, floating in front of the windshield. Her stereovision emerged intermittently, fleetingly, unexpectedly throughout the next day.

I sometimes receive calls, asking if amblyopia or strabismus treatment for adults can be successful.

"Is a person ever too old to get treatment for lazy eye?" they ask.

The answer: People of all ages can be treated for amblyopia and strabismus. The earlier the better still probably holds true. However, the definition of brain plasticity applies here. An individual of any age can change his/her brain. Vision therapy (VT) is brain-changing. In the Larkspur Landing Optometry office, I have worked with a number of amblyopia and strabismus patients—ages eleven, twenty, forty-three, fifty-nine, and younger.

Amblyopia and strabismus can be treated because the brain has "plasticity." The circuitry of the brain can actually change at any age. We use VT to retrain the visual system. This includes the eyes, the brain, and the visual pathways.

The website of the College of Optometrists in Vision Development (www.covd.org) explains the various treatments for amblyopia:

- Eyeglasses or contact lenses, where proper lenses can help reduce stress so that the underused eye can start to work more efficiently.

- Forcing the weaker eye to work by blocking or fogging the favored eye with special lenses, an eye patch, or eye drops
- A program of VT to help equalize vision in both eyes, improve eye coordination, and restore clear single vision

VT is probably most effective at an early age, but the plasticity of the brain can never be counted out. A person's visual system adapts so that it can function despite the person's visual limitations. Dr. Barry is a prime example. A neurobiologist, she managed to succeed in life despite her vision problems.

Many of you today are probably successful in your chosen careers, but the questions are: Do *you* want to try VT and see in 3-D? Do you always get headaches at 3-D movies? Do you want to train your brain to bring your turned eye or your lazy eye to clear vision?

I work with adult clients who have adapted and persevered despite their vision problems. Each of them is successful, but that does not mean it has been easy. We might see a college student who earns good grades but has to spend twice as much time studying as his/her peers. I have other clients who have read Susan Barry's book and just really want to see a snowflake or a leaf on a tree as she describes seeing them in her book. The younger clients want to see a 3-D movie as others experience it.

Scientists used to believe that a person could not recover his/her stereovision beyond the critical period of vision development, which is labeled at approximately ages two to eight. We now know the end of the critical period means that treatment of amblyopia will be more difficult, but certainly not impossible. In her book, Dr. Barry offers an amazing example of a person with strabismus who experiences the brain's plasticity at an older age.

Barry's anecdotal story is accompanied by references to scientific studies that indicate amblyopia can be treated in adulthood. As early as 1957, Carl Kupfer published a study in which he showed dramatic improvements in adults with amblyopia after a four-week period of eye-patching combined with VT. In a 1977 study, Martin Birnbaum and his colleagues reviewed twenty-three published studies on amblyopia and reported that improvements in eyesight were found for all ages. Sadly, these and other studies continue to be overlooked. Many doctors still believe that amblyopia can be treated only in young children.

The good news for adults with amblyopia is that there is a possibility for improved vision. However, there are no guarantees. Every case is different, and every patient must be thoroughly evaluated through a functional vision test. I encourage every reader to visit a developmental optometrist in order to begin any needed treatment. "Wake up and smell the roses" can easily change into "Wake up and see the snowflake!"

Another book I recommend reading is *Jillian's Story: How Vision Therapy Changed My Daughter's Life*, authored by Jillian's mother, Robin Benoit. As a former kindergarten teacher, I could visualize the "P" Day in Jillian's school that Robin describes. That day, the learners would be whispering the sound /p/ all day as they dressed in pirates' clothes, listening to stories containing lots of /p/ sounds, playing recognize-the-sound-of-"P" games, and practicing making the letter "P" with beans, glitter, and wallpaper.

What I cannot imagine is the absolute terror that Robin describes in her book. Screams came from Jillian as the teacher placed a pirate's patch over her eye. The little girl screamed that she could not see anything. She was acting as if she were blind.

Because Jillian had been born with limited vision in one eye, she had, since birth, always used only her strong eye. So technically she *was* blind in the other eye—but until that day, neither her parents nor her teachers had ever noticed that she was just using her brain for one eye.

That day started the journey for the Benoit family, who ultimately heard about and learned about VT. They made sure that Jillian engaged in VT until she regained her binocularity, depth perception and peripheral vision wearing corrective lenses.

Luckily, Jillian's story had a happy ending. She did not grow up with one eye/brain *never* seeing. But quite a few of you who are reading this book may actually be reading with only one eye. Sometimes the eye turn is intermittent or not noticeable. You may not know that you have amblyopia or strabismus if you have never been diagnosed.

Not everyone has amblyopia or strabismus. There are many visual skills deficiencies that require good binocular focus, especially for reading.

Another way to improve binocular focus is found in dedicated visual-skills computer programs, like the one I worked with at Gemstone Foundation (www.EyesInConflict.com). The computer program has five "games," or exercises, that the learner "plays" while trying to become proficient. In the fourth exercise, the learner must adjust his/her eyes to see the "hidden diamond figure" within the colored matrix dots. That exercise (Cross-Eyed Fusion) addresses convergence insufficiency. The fifth game (Wall-Eyed Fusion) works on divergence insufficiency. They train the eyes in teaming and turning, just as Dr. Barry and countless others have done when moving from near bead to far bead on the Brock string.

The five modules from the Eyes in Conflict program are listed below, along with the visual skill the exercise addresses:

1. **Fast focus (accommodation):** The eyes can adjust focus at different distances.

2. **Smooth tracking (pursuits):** The eyes can track a line of print from the beginning of the line to the end, and then return to the beginning of the next line.

3. **Jump tracking (saccades):** This is the length of time the eyes fixate on a word while reading.

4. **Cross-eyed fusion (convergence):** This is the ability of the eyes to turn inward and see objects (i.e., words) close up.

5. **Wall-eyed fusion (divergence):** This is the ability of the eyes to follow an object moving away.

The Gemstone Foundation, headed by Dr. Maureen Powers, PhD, FCOVD, FAAO, FARVO, is a non-profit funded primarily by NIH grants as well as local donors such as refineries and banks. The Foundation used the Eyes in Conflict program in four elementary schools in the Los Angeles Unified School District. The results are further evidence that students who improve their visual skills deficiencies also increase their reading ability. Dr. Powers collects the data from each child's first Convergence Insufficiency Symptom Survey (CISS) and assesses entry-level visual skills. Children are chosen who score high on the CISS and are below grade level in reading. In each school there are groups of thirty students at a time who then complete the Eyes in Conflict Dynamic Vision Training on the school's computers.

There have been some heartwarming stories from the parents of students whose reading improved so much in these Los Angeles Unified School District schools (see www.eyesinconflict.com). I suggest that everyone take the test at www.eyesinconflict.com and, if difficulties are identified, sign up for 30–100 of the exercises on the Internet program and make an appointment with a COVD Optometrist for vision therapy.

CLIENT SUCCESS

One summer, Dr. Powers met with the administration of the Rodeo Unified School District in northern California near where I worked as a vision therapist. Six to ten students who were "designated for assignment to Special Ed programs" were asked to take part in Gemstone Vision Dynamic Training throughout the summer. At the end of the program, none of the targeted kids that finished at least thirty sessions of the five modules had to be placed in Special Education classes.

In the Rodeo program the kids engaged for twenty to twenty-five minutes four days a week while Christy, my coworker, and I watched, oversaw, and helped. Two of the children—a brother and sister, JaySean and Melanie—made such dramatic improvement that they no longer needed to wear glasses. They are presently both excelling in school, and JaySean is on his high school's honor roll. Along with their mother, JaySean and Melanie have appeared numerous times before California State Senate Committees to speak about their Dynamic Vision Training, and their immediate improvements and long-term results. Their mother, Maryanne, who had never heard of VT before they participated in the program, feels that Gemstone Vision Dynamic Training saved her children's lives; that's why she and her children have taken the time to travel to Sacramento to tell their story. Here is a picture of them in front of the California State Capitol.

JaySean

JaySean started off relatively slowly, ascending the levels of the Eyes in Conflict program bit by bit. He attended regularly throughout the summer and had reached level 5 in four of the programs by mid-August. However, he could just not get his eyes to turn in for the convergence game four. JaySean worked on level one in Cross-Eyed Fusion for the entire summer. Finally, on August 20, he succeeded in moving to level two. I knew he was now on his way to finally changing his convergence insufficiency to convergence sufficiency. His two eyes would be able to team, turn inward, and allow his brain to "see" the words with both hemispheres. He would no longer have to strain his eye muscles by pulling his eyes back to the words when he read.

When Maryanne came to pick up the kids that day, I ran out to the car jumping up and down, hooting and hollering, "He did it! JaySean passed level one. He'll be able to focus on the words he is reading now! Woohoo!"

The kids thought I was nuts, but I knew he deserved a celebration. He had worked hard.

A few weeks later, Dr. Powers administered a post-test on JaySean using the Visagraph, an eye movement recording device that uses infrared light to track eye movements as a person reads a leveled reading prompt. The Visagraph provides a visual representation of the eye movements that can be printed out. Chills ran through my body as she held up JaySean's pre-test and post-test charts next to each other. Indeed, I could see how his right eye had veered off in his first Visagraph, with lots of regressions and re-readings. Now, this hard-working eleven-year-old exclaimed, "Wow, my eyes followed the words line for line today, not like all that skipping lines and re-reading words at the beginning of the summer."

Melanie

Melanie indeed came a long way with the Gemstone DVT program. I cannot forget the first week in Rodeo, with Melanie sitting in front of the computer trying to hold the accommodative lens flippers in front of her eyes. Her hand shook so much the lenses couldn't sit still on her nose. For a number of weeks, Christy held the flippers for her so she could practice the accommodative skill.

During different points in the summer, Melanie, too, had progressed to the highest level on four of the modules. Her shaky hand had subsided as her skills strengthened, and she was now able to use flippers five and six to finish off the accommodation module and move through level five. However, she was stuck on level one of Jump Tracking. We knew this skill, if mastered, would make reading so much easier for her.

On September 9th, Melanie had finally trained her eyes/brain enough to pass from level one to level two in Jump Tracking. When her mom's car arrived, I repeated my high school cheerleader-like jumping and yelling, crying out, "She did it! She did it! She passed Jump Tracking!"

I knew Melanie's hard work all summer had finally paid off. She would be able to track across a line of print, seeing the words as she read.

Sebas

Another young boy with whom I worked in Guatemala also met with success during the training we did together. Although Sebas originally was referred to me for his ADHD, I could tell that he also had some vision issues.

I recognized his numerous behavior difficulties at his school as overlapping ADHD behaviors and low visual skills behaviors. As part of the first-day protocol, I asked Sebas to stand on the balance board while following the heart at the end of a pencil with his eyes as I moved it. He was not using both eyes. Especially when I brought the heart to his nose, one eye barely budged. I asked his mother to call an eye doctor to schedule an eye exam.

Sebas came back the next week with a patch over one eye, plus a warning that if he did not wear it for six weeks, his one eye might never work. Sebas wanted one of my Raiders patches, a plastic one, so he would not have to wear a "band aid" type every day. He had exactly the same problem as Jillian in the book *Jillian's Story*: as had been the case with Jillian, no one had noticed that during his young life, one of his eyes had done all the work of seeing and his brain had just quit working with his other eye.

I am happy to report that Sebas brought his "lazy eye" back online as a result of patching in less than six weeks.

I worked at Larkspur Landing Optometry in Larkspur, CA for four years. Each of the following patients gained tremendously from vision therapy (VT) and successfully graduated from VT, passing the optometrist's visual skills exams.

Bo

As a young boy, Bo had four operations to straighten his turned eye so his eyes looked matched. At age nineteen, he read Dr. Sue Barry's book *Fixing My Gaze* and realized that if he pursued VT like Dr. Barry, he might be able to see in 3-D too. Therefore, he asked his dad if he would let him proceed with VT at Larkspur Landing Optometry. Bo had read of this woman, who, like him, had operations as a child to straighten an eye but who was never able to use that straightened eye correctly to see in 3-D. As Bo was a teenage movie buff, he longed to see 3-D movies with the 3-D glasses handed out at the movie theater doors. However, he knew his surgically straightened eye was not allowing him to do that—yet.

Bo was a delight with whom to work. I learned a lot from him. For example, it was interesting to use the Wheatstone apparatus, which some people call "the bat." Two small mirrors are located close to the nose, on the middle tip of the "W" shape. The patient is supposed to move the "wings" until s/he can see the target while looking into the mirrors. The first time I was working with Bo, I asked, "Do you see fish in the bowl?" which usually indicated the two eyes were teaming to converge the two images. Bo answered "yes." Then I looked at his eyes. He was looking straight ahead at the fish with his left eye, and at the bowl with his right eye. This was a typical response for a non-dominant-eyed individual who for years had used his eyes separately, but it was not practicing convergence. As VT progressed, so did Bo's ability to look into the mirrors and see the targets using the mirrors with convergence.

In addition to his success with the Wheatstone apparatus, Bo was excited after watching the 3-D movie *Gravity*. He actually borrowed some prism lenses from the optometry office to aid his 3-D viewing. Afterward he called me on the phone, excitedly telling me how he saw the water drip come out of the faucet in the movie. There were other movies and other 3-D experiences for Bo, but I will always remember his excitement about that drop of water.

Bo's story confirmed for me the importance of individuals accessing the expertise of a developmental optometrist if they have had operations for turned-in eye.

Nate

Nate came to vision therapy at Larkspur Landing Optometry at age eleven. His grandmother had noticed something "different" about Nate's eye when he was about two years old. Since that time, his parents had taken him to ophthalmologists and optometrists. His mom stated that he had worn glasses since he was twenty-two months old and had used patches for varying amounts of time during his early years. Neither ophthalmologist had ever recommended surgery.

Nate's mom, Robin, researched vision therapy on the Internet. None of the doctors who had examined Nate had ever recommended VT. When Nate began complaining that he was continuously seeing double, his mom made the appointment that really changed his vision and his outlook on life. It turned out that Nate had been seeing double for quite some time, but his parents were unaware.

Nate's "breakthrough experience" was receiving prism lenses in his glasses from Dr. Day. During VT, Nate practiced using 20-degree prisms and 14-degree prisms. He took them home and used them for more than an hour each day. He adjusted well; he did not complain at all about using them.

One of the experiences Nate especially enjoyed was using the 20-degree prisms at a 3-D movie. He usually got headaches at 3-D movies and could not see the images in three dimensions. But with the prisms, he could. He was totally amazed at what he was seeing. He grabbed at the images as they appeared to pop off the screen. "That's so cool," was his repeated phrase throughout the movie. Nate's mom was so happy she cried.

Nate also used two computer programs for homework while he was working in VT. Both programs made his weaker eye much stronger. As his left eye improved, so did his binocularity skills. He is now an accomplished skier and mountain biker, both of which improved with the development of his depth perception.

There is an exercise we perform in VT that sums up my experience with Nate. The exercise entails holding the small, rectangular Vectogram quoits (rope circles on a clear plastic sheet) in front of one's face in a BI (base in) position while wearing polaroid lenses. Then I swing the Pendulum Ball toward the quoits. Usually, the learner is awed as the ball approaches. The person feels that the ball is coming through the plastic in a tube-like cylinder view. I have never had a child or adult patient who did not love this activity—until Nate.

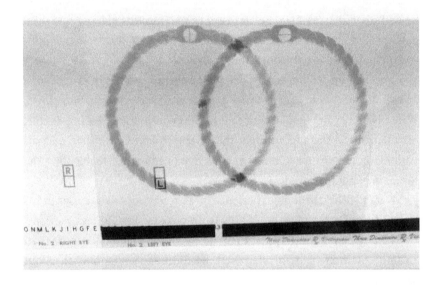

Nate had worked on the Vectogram device with Polaroid glasses in Base In and Base Out exercises. The doctor thought he was ready to try this cool technique, too. But, when Nate held the quoits in his hands, he cried. It hurt so much to see him and hear him. Tears flowed down his face as he said, "I can never do this. I see double everything. I see two quoits, not one. I see two balls on the string." He was despondent. And why is this my marker for Nate? Because before he graduated from VT, he could actually see only one quoit and see the "tunnel" that the ball appeared to come through. He succeeded in his binocularity development so much that he was able to do this particular exercise that had originally brought him (and me) so much pain.

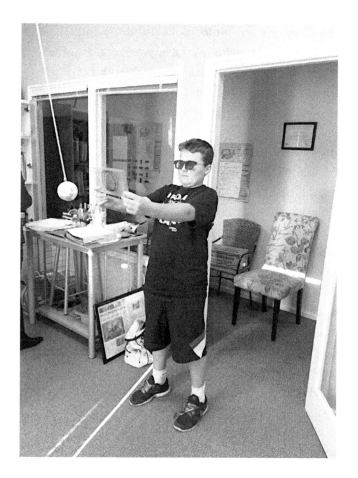

When Nate left VT, he wore glasses made with 6-degree prisms. These greatly aided his ability to read the board and books, and to maintain a high grade point average in middle school.

All of these patients received vision therapy, which I recommend for anyone with strabismus or amblyopia.

ACTION GUIDE

The first action you should take is to sign up for an assessment at www. eyesinconflict.com under the heading "Eyes Together Training." Then the Gemstone Foundation will send you the appropriate materials needed in order to perform an assessment of your child's visual skills on their website.

Brain Bag Activities (for motor skills development): The brain bag is about four inches square, with four tablespoons of rice inside. Perform all the activities about ten times each: first with both hands together, then using same hand, then left to right, then right to left. It is important to keep eyes on the brain bag throughout its trajectory.

- Throw above head and catch.
- Throw and lightly touch ceiling and catch.
- Throw as close to ceiling as possible without touching and catch.
- Throw a foot away from ceiling and catch.
- While moving on walking rail, toss bag hand to hand, hand to hand as if beating a drum, bring bag around the body both ways, and place on head.

Fill in the Loops: If your child has difficulty with directionality/laterality on the trampoline, sit with a page in a book or magazine and have your child color in the loops of letters (a, b, d, g, p, q)—those facing the right in red, and those facing left in blue. Once s/he can do that well, instead of filling in the loops, have him/her tell you which color s/he would have used in the loop.

Fruit Loops: Practice moving a pipe cleaner into fruit loops. Be sure the "needle point" of the pipe cleaner is going *into* the cereal. The child is not to place fruit loops *onto* the pipe cleaner. That is important. Can make bracelets.

Games and Activities: See Chapter 3 Action Guide.

Geoboard: A geoboard is a square piece of wood with nails evenly spaced in rows. Use rubber bands over the nails to stretch into shapes. Use two boards and have the child copy the pattern you make on the board. The child must use the same nails you used to make the pattern. You can practice many visual skills. For visual memory, show your board and then remove it so child needs to form the pattern from memory. Make a pattern on your board and have the child make a mirror image on his/her geoboard. Start with two rubber bands. Then use four. Continue to add two rubber bands as the child's skills strengthen.

Mini-Trampoline (for laterality and processing): Draw arrows on a piece of paper going in left, right, up, and down directions and place on wall. The child jumps rhythmi-cally on trampoline and reads the arrows, pushing air with his/her arms in the direction of the arrows while saying the name of the direction. The learner can also call and do opposite of the directions. A variation is to mix the direction arrows on a sheet of paper with two animals, such as a pig and duck. Then the child must read the sheet aloud while jump-ing, but make the appropriate sound of the animals as well as say the arrow directions.

Near Far: Use parquetry blocks. Take the blocks from box and mix up. Place one of the design sheets across the room. Have child re-create the design in the bottom of the box from a distance. (Child will need to look up and down, back and forth to complete the design.)

Pencil Push-Ups: See Chapter 3 Action Guide.

Starfish: See Chapter 2 Action Guide.

Visual Memory Game: Use three visually distinct objects or three colored blocks or three different-shaped blocks and a manila folder. Show the child the three objects lined up in order. Then hide them with the folder. Ask the child to name the objects in order.

I hope you enjoyed these Action Guide activities. The Pencil Push-Up is probably the most important to practice. Patients with amblyopia or strabismus may find the activities very difficult, but with perseverance, they can experience quantifiable progress.

CHAPTER 5:

The Belgau Work

I WAS WORKING WITH YOUNG people in my Brain Ways office before I learned the formal techniques and exercises for visual development to assist patients in vision therapy (VT). Those early kids were developing their visual skills too, but at the time, I was like many of the readers of this book: I did not know much about VT. It turned out that every adult and child with whom I worked was actually doing exercises in vision development, however, because I was using equipment developed by Dr. Frank Belgau in every session.

Belgau created some very specific balancing equipment in the 1970s, while he was teaching at the College of Optometry in Houston, and he focused on vision skills as he developed his program, which he called the Learning Breakthrough Program. I have used the Learning Breakthrough Program since day one. Every adult and child with whom I worked spent more than half of the session using equipment developed by Belgau to integrate their left and right hemispheres, augment their neuropathways, and develop their vision.

When I completed my first course in 2005 with Dr. Belgau and his wife, Beverly, there were thirty to thirty-five participants. We progressed from station to station, performing various tasks and recording our results. Then we engaged in activities on Belgau Boards for about thirty minutes. After working with the Belgau apparatus, each participant returned to the stations to repeat those opening activities.

There were three specific station activities that demonstrated the impact of the Belgau Platform Board activities on my own visual system.

The first one required reading a chart on the wall. We were asked to focus on lines on the chart while walking backwards slowly, and to stop when the lines became blurry. The floor was taped with measurements marking the distance from the wall. When I repeated that procedure after working on the Belgau Board, I noticed that my distance from the chart had increased quite a bit.

The second activity was one in which a deck of playing cards was laid out, face up, on a table. Our task required us to focus on the card in the very middle, and then look out into our periphery and write down the cards that we could recognize. When we returned to that station after our other activities, many of us found that we could see further by a row or two and column or two than our original view of the cards. To many, the cards also appeared brighter and easier to read.

The third post-test station activity involved reading a similar paragraph to one we had read before beginning the Belgau protocols. The task required reading the paragraph out loud into a small digital recorder. After we recorded the second reading, we were able to listen to both recordings. Of the entire class, there was only one man who did not think his oral reading the second time was better than the first. Of course, the brain process of reading aloud was probably improved via our balance board work. I am positing that the visual system also made improvements, such that the reading after the activities was "easier," more "free-flowing."

From my training, and from working with various pieces of Dr. Belgau's proprietary equipment, I learned that both visual processing and auditory processing must travel through the vestibular before arriving at separate areas of the brain. When a learner is standing on a Belgau Board,

I know s/he is maintaining his/her balance by using the vestibular. Then we "challenge" the vestibular by changing the rockers on the board, hitting the Pendulum Ball, and aiming at targets several feet away. (In VT, we call this adding of tasks "loading.") I insist the learner take turns with the right side, then the left side so the neural pathways being used traverse the brain.

Dr. Belgau explains the importance of Pendulum Ball exercises:

> In activities 14–25, your hands were used in a lot of ways to hit and control the movement of the Pendulum Ball through space. Each change in the way the hands were held to hit the ball required a different program to be generated and executed in the brain. All of the activities had a lot in common, but each one was unique in some way. The advantage of this kind of activity is that a much more elaborate structure must be built in the brain to control the motion of the Pendulum Ball while hitting it in all the different ways. This principle is a very important one in developing activities that organize the brain and in developing higher levels of operation. (2001, 10)

Dr. Belgau's exercises with the Visual Motor Control Stick (VMCS) build in the left-right-left-right procedure through the use of numbers and colors that stand for varying distances from the center of the stick. If a person is alternating hitting bars of the same color, then s/he is hitting in the L-R-L-R sequence. What has improved as a result of this sequencing? By exercising motor skills, one's brain is stimulated to develop communication pathways from left hemisphere to right hemisphere and vice-versa. In addition, back-to-front-to back pathways are formed that ultimately improve visual functioning.

Functional vision is the foundation of good visual perceptual skills. Visual perceptual skills are the way the brain processes what the eyes see. They are like a feedback loop in a computer system. The eyes are the keyboard, the brain is the computer, and the hands are the printer. If the keyboard or input system is not working correctly, the computer cannot receive and process the correct information effectively. Thus, the printer will not print the correct output. This analogy is easily equated to the child who is having difficulty in kicking a ball while running, as well as experiencing handwriting challenges at any age.

There are many different types of visual perceptual skills, including: visual memory, visual closure, visual discrimination, visual figure ground, visual-spatial relations, and visual form constancy. In the VT office, we evaluate levels of these perceptual skills and work on improving weak ones. In my practice, I did not focus specifically on "visual skills," but many of my Structure of Intellect (SOI) activities required them. Therefore, as the children progressed through the modules, they progressively developed their visual perceptual skills as well.

Then, in February 2008, a friend, Maria, gave me a marvelous book, written by Dr. Kenneth Lane, DO, FCOVD, entitled *Success for Your Child in School*. The book emphasized the development of visual perceptual skills for school success and listed hundreds of activities. Also, I had been a kindergarten teacher for many years, so I already knew the how-to

for development of skills. I simply had not knowingly incorporated the development of visual skills, visual perceptual skills, and vision therapy when I initiated Brain Ways.

Even before I acquired knowledge of vision therapy, I was using Brain Ways activities that assisted my clients in developing convergence and divergence vision skills. For example, in Dr. Belgau's exercises with the VMCS, the learner hits the Pendulum Ball at a spot on the VMCS (convergence) and watches the ball as it moves away toward the target (divergence). Directions for this activity include: Aim to swing over and back above the diamond target. Place hands, palms down, on the green bars of the VMCS. Hit the ball alternating on the numerals 3 and 6, on the red bars. Watch the ball as it hits on the correct numeral and then watch the ball as it goes away from you toward the targets. Does the Pendulum Ball go toward the intended target? If not successful, make adjustments on your next swing (Belgau 2004, 4).

Just like exercises in the VT room at the optometrist's office, these exercises help develop convergence and divergence skills, with the added bonus of being on a balance board challenging the vestibular.

Another important visual skill is peripheral vision, the part of vision that occurs outside the very center of the gaze. When I began studying vision therapy, I bought a Marsden Ball, which hangs from the ceiling, pendulum-style, and has capital letters and numerals printed on it. At the office of the vision therapist I was observing, I watched children and adults lying on the floor, following the ball with their eyes horizontally, vertically, diagonally, and around their face in a circle. Sometimes the vision therapist would have the child stand on a balance board and swing the ball around the child's body at different heights. The learner would either name the letters they saw or look for the letters the vision therapist called out. I understood the ball-around-the-body was working on peripheral vision skills.

Dr. Belgau's *Pendulum Ball Manual* (2001) lists activities learners engage in that are very similar to activities practiced in VT. The first forty-two exercises in the manual start with exactly the same exercises patients in VT perform, in fact. Directions from the Pendulum Ball Manual, Belgau, page 1, include:

1. *Track the ball as it swings horizontally from left to right and back from right to left.*
2. *Track the ball as it swings vertically from top to bottom and back from bottom to top.*
3. *Track the ball as it swings in a clockwise direction.*

And so it continues, with Pendulum Ball exercises using the Belgau ball instead of a Marsden ball for the eyes, just like in a VT session in an optometrist's office, until the last exercise in the list of activities: *42. Use a flashlight or headlight to track the ball in various ways.*

In addition to visual motor skills, Dr. Belgau also explains and provides exercises in which the Pendulum Ball provides a framework of activities for developing body image and organizing the child's physical system using Pendulum Ball activities (2001). Using an assessment similar to these activities, I evaluate most of my clients for body awareness and may work with them to improve their visual skills through use of Belgau's Platform Balance Board, using his Pendulum Ball, targets, and Visual Motor Control Stick (VMCS); or on a balance board (also called a walking rail), along with a Rotation Board for further vestibular (balance and equilibrium) development.

CLIENT SUCCESS

Jacob

I had a new-for-me experience with one client, Jacob. When asked to name parts of his body being touched by a pointer, Jacob named totally unrelated, random body parts. For example, with his eyes closed, lying on the floor, the pointer touched his right shoulder, then his left knee, followed by his right foot. When Jacob said, "right hand, right ear, and left elbow," I truly thought he was joking, kidding me. I tried a sequence on one side: right foot, right hand, right shoulder, but he did no better. I had read of proprioception, but never known a client with this total lack of body awareness. I quickly changed from accusing him of trying to trick me to accepting that I was having a "first time in my life" experience. This was my introduction to body awareness, known as proprioception.

Jacob worked on naming body parts and on various other skills twice a week on the Belgau Board and made great progress. By the end of his time at Brain Ways, Jacob definitely had a sense of where he was in space, and even passed a variation of that first day test with eyes closed with flying colors. His ability to run and kick a ball also improved. VT helped me appreciate how very important body awareness is to the visual system and other skills that a child lacks. No wonder Jacob had trouble kicking a ball!

Since that first experience, I have worked with many patients in VT on body contact. We perform exercises in which they tap different parts of their bodies with the Pendulum Ball. Using Brain Ways activities, Jacob had to spend a long time hitting the ball with different body parts. Jacob had a hard time tossing the rice brain bag from one hand to another. He was also unable to catch a bag that was thrown to him, even from a short distance, by me. However, with the Pendulum Ball, we could discuss laterality and reinforce names of body parts as he tapped the ball. He did not have to catch it; it would not fall. He could just tap the ball shoulder—right elbow or left knee, for example—and the names could be reinforced. The increased vestibular challenge of being on the balance board required Jacob to establish a higher level of integration of the various parts of his body and his visual system, according to Dr. Belgau. Together, my knowledge of VT and Dr. Belgau's exercises have been extremely beneficial for my clients.

Ceci

I had asked that Ceci make an appointment at the local Guatemalan ophthalmologist after her SOI assessment results indicated her visual skills and eyesight needed to be checked. The doctor found some visual skills deficiencies, and scheduled her for some VT in his clinic. However, Ceci only attended two or three sessions. "Flexibility" was one visual skill Dr. L. diagnosed as weak in Ceci's functional vision test. Instead of continuing VT with him, Ceci engaged in Brain Ways' entire program of TLP music, Belgau Board Activities, Brain Gym®, and SOI modules.

Now, as I write this book, I realize how much Ceci's visual skills deficiencies improved. Visualizing her on the Belgau Board, I think that of all the areas we practiced, it was Ceci's increasing superiority on the board, with the Pendulum Ball, targets, and use of the VMCS, that aided her visual skills development. I had never had a student before, nor have I since, who worked so diligently on the Belgau Board.

I spoke years later with Ceci, as this book was heading for publication. I wanted her permission to use her story. "Oh, yes," she replied. "Before I worked with you, I would read [right brain] but could not remember [left brain] what I read. After I worked with you, I recalled what I read, which made school so much easier. That's why I did so well in school and life after working at Brain Ways."

Miguel

I loved Miguel's enthusiasm for just about everything. When he heard from me, for example, that an eleven-year-old girl could turn all the way around, a 360-degree turn, on the Rotation Board in just two moves, he immediately began practicing on the Rotation Board in order to compete with Catherine's accomplishment. This was a very good drill for Miguel because his vestibular needed work. I never needed to cajole or encourage him to work on the balance boards—he always wanted to best Catherine's latest feat. Most of my students performed six to eight turns to get all the way around on the Rotation Board. I never told Miguel as he progressed from eight turns to two that Catherine had passed all my vestibular tests with flying colors; she had no deficits in her ability to balance.

Miguel's mother reported that after we finished about six months of working together at Brain Ways, she noticed something very interesting: Miguel's peripheral vision and his balance were both much improved. Miguel always was and still is a risk taker. It is part of his makeup. His attributes assessment with the Structure of Intellect (SOI) showed that Miguel had high creativity but was not so adept in the evaluative realm. This is actually quite common for many teenagers, as the pre-frontal cortex, the area of the brain where executive decisions such as evaluating are made, is not fully developed. In Miguel's case, his high creativity and lower evaluative skills showed up in the form of scrapes and bruises as he was also quite low in his peripheral visual skills. His mother reported that he was her one child who always seemed to walk into bushes and fall off ledges and play structures. After his work on his visual skills in Brain Ways, however, she noticed that his scrapes from branches during their walks in the woods decreased dramatically. And although he has continued his risk-taking behaviors to some extent, she has noticed quite a decrease in traumatic results. Instead, Miguel has shown good balance in sports that he had tried before but had failed to master, such as surfing.

The nicest conversation happened just as this book was heading to publication, so I want to add a recap: I happened to be in Guatemala, and Miguel What'sApped me from Spain, where he is working now that he's graduated from the Hotel Management School. He had just begun reading a book about the brain and was intrigued by all he was learning. "What was all that brain stuff you did with me on all those wooden boards?" he asked. "And, Betsy, I read so many books now. I never read a book before you worked with me. Now I am always reading two books at the same time, every month!"

It was heartwarming to know that the kid who used to *not* read was not only reading but enjoying it. To add to my joy at what I was hearing, Miguel added, "Thank you, Betsy. I know what I did in your office really changed me for the better. I love learning so much from books."

ACTION GUIDE

This chapter contains no formal Action Guide because the way to work the activities featured in it is to order the apparatus from www.balametrics.com. Once you have at least the Platform Balance Board, the Pendulum Ball, the Visual Motor Control Stick, the target stand, and targets, you can commence the activities and hence the Action Guide for this section. The equipment comes with manuals describing exactly what to perform and why.

CHAPTER 6:

Structure of Intellect

SOI STANDS FOR STRUCTURE OF INTELLECT—a theory of the functions and products of human intelligence on which a system of tests and booklets for assessing and developing intellectual abilities is based. SOI is based on the work of J.P. Guilford, whose search for intellectual abilities began in 1940 and whose original purpose in designing the test was to aid the US Armed Services in finding pilots with the right aptitudes to learn to fly airplanes. The US had entered World War II and needed fighter pilots. Originally, the US Armed Services used IQ scores as an entrance to the pilot program. The flunk-out rate was so high—near 50 percent—that obviously high IQ did not predict piloting skills. Hence, the government commissioned a study by Guilford.

Dr. Mary Meeker worked with Guilford in the 1960s and winnowed down the many aptitudes of his original test to the twenty-four used for educational purposes today. Specifically, she applied the theory of human intelligence into a practical, usable program that identifies levels of abilities required for learning and then offers training to improve those levels. She was most interested in applying Guilford's theory to education. Her husband, Dr. Robert Meeker, and others at SOI have continued to use the theory of intelligence as a basis for developing new modules.

Mary Meeker defines the SOI method for success as follows:

1. Identify the abilities required for the learning of reading, arithmetic, math, or requisites for any given job.

2. Test for those abilities.

3. Teach abilities which are low, maintain those which are gifted, and develop further any that are average.

4. Compare levels of performance with and without SOI training to document the difference it can make.

This approach makes traditional education much more successful. (Meeker and Meeker 1978, 2)

I, and other practitioners, use the many modules that Dr. Meeker developed with our learners to identify clients' strengths and teach to their weaknesses, as well as to develop their self-esteem. A learning disability is simply the absence of a learning ability. Intelligence can be trained. Everyone has intelligence. The question is not, "How much?" (like an IQ); the question is, "What kind?" Many who feel like "non-learners" in school are really simply "learning-different." There is hope.

When Brain Ways acquires a new client/student, I use the SOI assessment to assess in the twenty-four SOI abilities that underlie school curricula. From other chapters of this book, you learn of the other apparati and exercises I use with my students. Concurrently, I work diligently with them to teach the SOI aptitudes.

For some of the modules, I have computer programs, provided by SOI Systems, with which I work one-on-one with the students. With the computer modules, the kids receive immediate feedback, such as in "Getting from Here to There." As part of this module, a learner is to find the shortest path between A and D. The learner may click on A to G to C to E to D. If s/he has found the shortest path, the computer sentence reads: "You have found the shortest path." If there is a shorter path, then the computer reads: "There is a shorter path." Thus, the learner has immediate feedback and tries to find the shortest route right away.

SOI AND VISION

There is a sentence in the printout of the SOI test results that states, "if your assessment shows you are low in CFU or NST (or other vision-related subtests) then an examination is needed by a developmental or behavioral optometrist" (Meeker 2007, 5). The day I first read that, I think I was in the same place as many readers of this book and many parents who have come to me in my role as Vision Therapist. When I sent my very first clients to a developmental optometrist, I did not know the difference between "eyesight" and "vision" either (see Chapter 3).

SOI provides an "SOI Vision Form" pamphlet for all practitioners to use as a follow-up to SOI assessments. The form includes an outline for Vision Indicators, Behavioral Indicators, and a Vision Examination, as well as a Treatment Plan graph.

Statements from the SOI Vision Form pamphlet are very revealing.

Vision Indicators: "SOI assessments are not vision tests, but as authors of the assessment, we are aware that some of the SOI tests require greater vision skills than others. . . . [W]hen low, we want to alert those who are receiving the results of the assessment, that vision may be a contributing factor to learning problems" (Robert Meeker, 2007). And, indeed, from my experience, oftentimes when a parent has brought me a child with learning difficulties, the SOI has confirmed some low levels on the foundational abilities for reading or some other visual-related SOI area.

Behavioral Indicators: "Those who know the client personally can provide some very helpful information relating to the client's behavior that may be influenced by vision." The SOI Vision Behavioral Checklist helps in that area, as parents, teachers, and learners themselves can attest to; this type of feedback can include "inclining head," "loses place when reading," "omits small words," "is unable to copy," and "draws without angles." Many behaviors on the checklist are indicators or telltale signs of a vision or visual skills deficiency.

A number of Subtests in the SOI assessment provide vision-related results:

- **CFU**: Visual closure
- **CFT**: Visual perspective
- **MSU**: Visual attending
- **MSS**: Visual sequencing
- **EFU**: Visual discrimination
- **NFU**: Psycho-motor skills
- **NST**: Speed of word recognition
- **DMU**: Margin tendency, spelling, handwriting

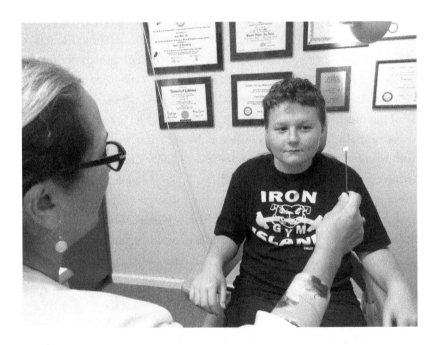

The best thing about SOI's list of related-to-vision subtests is that there are modules of work that strengthen the subtest's skills with paper and pencil or computer work.

I believe the Examination Chart provided by SOI for patients to bring to the developmental optometrist is priceless. The markings indicate where the person scores on a spectrum that ranges from UNSKILLED to MARGINAL to SKILLED. The second instruction states to the doctor, "Record your findings of the visual exam below." A Vision Therapist, as well as a parent or patient, can then see very clearly which skills fall in what location on the spectrum. The form works as a very graphic representation of pre- and post-skills, allowing clients to see their own growth when they have a progress check with the optometrist.

The list of skills on the Examination Chart include:

- Eye movement skills, including pursuit, saccadic fixation, and convergence.
- Eye focusing skills, including amplitude, flexibility, and acuity.
- Eye teaming skills, including binocular alignment, focus alignment, stereopsis/suppression, and form perception.

(Note: see Glossary of Terms for definitions and explanations of skills)

Vision skills are inherently important in educational settings. Having taught kindergarten and first grade for more than twenty years, I was well aware of the importance of tracking in reading. Tracking requires the two eyes to move together from the left side of the page, following the words in a horizontal line to the right. When I saw the modules with the open eyes with directions to move the eyes horizontally or vertically, I knew my students needed to work through these pages. The first pages of the module had practice for the two eyes to work together, looking at the first open-eyes icon and then moving one's own eyes in vertical or horizontal directions.

Another component of tracking is called "saccades." In this SOI module, each time a client stops to read or say the number of the eye printed on the page, it comprises a saccade.

The vertical saccade practice gives the first sound (or letter) at the top of a column of word endings. The exercise requires moving one's eyes

Instructions: In this exercise, move from EYEPOINT #1 to #2 to #3 to #4 to #5. Under each EYE-POINT is a word or letter(s). Read the letter under EYEPOINT #1 then move to #2. If the letters at EYE-POINT #2 make a real word when combined with the letter in EYEPOINT #1, check the "Y" box. If not, check the "N" box. The first row is done for you.

Pronounce the two sounds of each word as the student does the visual tracking.

Always go from #1 to #2, back to #1 then to #3, back to #1 then to #4, back to #1 finally to #5.

EYEPOINTS 1-5

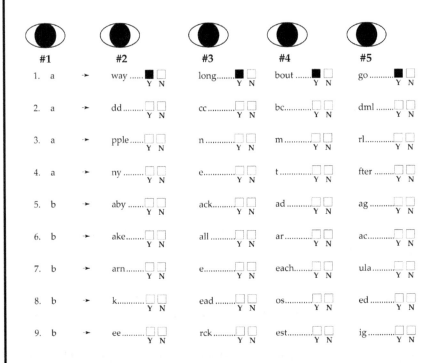

#1		#2	#3	#4	#5
1.	a	way ...... ■ ☐ Y N	long....... ■ ☐ Y N	bout ...... ■ ☐ Y N	go .... ■ ☐ Y N
2.	a	dd .... ☐ ☐ Y N	cc .... ☐ ☐ Y N	bc............. ☐ ☐ Y N	dml .... ☐ ☐ Y N
3.	a	pple ...... ☐ ☐ Y N	n .... ☐ ☐ Y N	m .... ☐ ☐ Y N	rl.............. ☐ ☐ Y N
4.	a	ny .... ☐ ☐ Y N	e .... ☐ ☐ Y N	t .... ☐ ☐ Y N	fter .... ☐ ☐ Y N
5.	b	aby ...... ☐ ☐ Y N	ack........... ☐ ☐ Y N	ad .... ☐ ☐ Y N	ag .... ☐ ☐ Y N
6.	b	ake........ ☐ ☐ Y N	all .... ☐ ☐ Y N	ar............. ☐ ☐ Y N	ac............ ☐ ☐ Y N
7.	b	arn........ ☐ ☐ Y N	e .... ☐ ☐ Y N	each........ ☐ ☐ Y N	ula.......... ☐ ☐ Y N
8.	b	k............. ☐ ☐ Y N	ead .... ☐ ☐ Y N	os............. ☐ ☐ Y N	ed .... ☐ ☐ Y N
9.	b	ee .... ☐ ☐ Y N	rck.......... ☐ ☐ Y N	est............ ☐ ☐ Y N	ig .... ☐ ☐ Y N

Review: If students do not read, but can understand spoken vocabulary, read the EYEPOINT focus sound and each word aloud. Pronounce the two parts of the word aloud as the student makes the eye movements.

The sounds, when read aloud, may sound like a word. (Repeat page 1 before going on to next page.)

NSR-I

quickly from the first letter to the given ending in the column, stating "yes" or "no" if the letters together make a word, then returning the eyes' gaze back to the top and repeating the process. The client then progresses down the columns, looking for real words in each column. My clients and I did a similar exercise in VT to improve flexibility.

The horizontal saccade exercises similarly listed either the first or last letter. The student would read the beginnings or endings across the page, saying "yes" or "no" if the first letter and the endings made a word.

Although the paper module leaves little boxes by the "yes" and "no" to mark the correct answer, I prefer to do the exercises orally, so the student can concentrate on the saccades and pursuits of his/her eye movements.

In addition to tracking, a number of other SOI modules require very fine discrimination between pictures to accomplish the tasks and complete the modules. These attention-to-detail activities also refine the visual system processes. Some students are under-convergent, for example, others are over-convergent, and still others are already spot-on with their convergence. Each time they practice in the discrimination modules, all are practicing their vergence skills.

CLIENT SUCCESS

I cannot think of a child with whom I have worked who has not benefited from the SOI modules. Each child works individually with me on the modules ascertained from his/her SOI assessment results. In the following stories, I will mention a number of the various modules with which my children have worked.

Alberto

In addition to the SOI computer modules, there are paper-pencil modules to complete. Kids invariably like the pages and computer programs that are easier for them to complete. We do them all anyway. I work with a learner who is on the autistic spectrum who really loves the "Semantic Maze." If he could, he would spend his entire hour with me trying to locate five sequential words in Semantic Maze. But we have Brain Gym®, Belgau Board, Integrated Listening Systems, and the Active 8 on the wall waiting for some left-right brain integration, as well as other modules, both paper and computer. So the Semantic Maze has become his reward. If he works on other modules and completes his active brain work, then he gets to do Semantic Maze toward the end of his session. Alberto works diligently and is making good progress.

Alex

There are modules for all of the abilities, and levels within the aptitudes as well. I will just mention a few, so the reader can get a feeling for what completing a module entails. The DMU, or Divergent seMantic Units, involve creative writing. Alex wrote creative stories using the prompts of descriptive and creative words that went along with pictures of unusual animals. Every child brings his/her own divergent thinking to this task. Sometimes we would need to look up the animal online, as we were not familiar with it (the eland, for example). Our discoveries led to a lesson in habitats and continents as well.

Ajna and Isiah

Ajna and Isiah, two preteens in Brain Ways, worked on Cognition of seMantic Systems (CMS). If this ability is well developed, the learner is better able to understand complicated verbal information. This skill, which is an underlying ability for understanding instructions, was important to both learners, as Ajna wanted to star in musical theater and Isiah wanted to be the best basketball player he could be. The module contained thirteen exercises that involved comprehension of a series of ideas or concepts. The young learners looked upon the exercises as a sort of mystery tour in which they tried to follow the directions to find the correct answer. With some practice, I would say both learners quite enjoyed the exercises in the module. Ajna's mother reported that the following year of school was more successful than the previous one. Ajna performed in a couple of shows that next year, too. Isiah joined the varsity-level basketball team at his middle school.

Ceci

Some of Ceci's lowest SOI levels were in semantics, so we worked on what I called Vocabulary modules. This could have been a torturous exercise for a kid who had flunked a couple of times, but we somehow made it through many modules. The first modules contain pictures where the learner has to find matching words that describe the object or activity in the picture. Ceci liked these a lot better than the words on the left side that had to be matched with definitions or descriptions on the right. She was successful as we worked on harder and higher levels. Most of my Guatemalan students worked many semantic modules with me. For the most part, I worked with English vocabulary with my clients, and the learners would often translate the word into Spanish and be able to describe the meaning in Spanish as well.

Diego

Diego's Structure of Intellect (SOI) aptitudes test showed that a fourth of his aptitudes were in the low range, another quarter was in the genius range, and the rest were in the average range. We worked on various SOI modules that seemed to raise his self-esteem as he finished them, as well as give him a good foundation for all of his learning. We worked initially on his lowest scores, through the average aptitudes and then through his gifted levels. I am sure his success in school that followed was, at least in part, a result of him having completed so many of those SOI modules.

Isiah and Alex

Both Isiah and Alex concentrated on using verbal relations in the Cognition of seMantic Relations (CMR) module, as in analogies. It was interesting for me to work with two boys of nearly the same age but with distinct differences in their learning styles. Isiah preferred to work together orally with me, discussing the differences among the objects. Alex's style was more contemplative and quiet. They both needed to develop this underlying skill, however. They each did so, working their way through drawings of fat pencils, thin paint brushes, the first, then the last, then the third item, and so on. Both boys engaged in this and a number of symbolic modules, both in paper and pencil and on the computer. Both sets of parents reported how much "easier" math class seemed to be for them in the following year of school. Although the boys were in different schools, both of them received high grades in their math classes following their completion of the modules.

I have had great fun and excellent results throughout the years with SOI. For my clients, engaging in SOI modules has provided them with the opportunity to more greatly meet their full potential.

ACTION GUIDE

In order to have SOI modules to work with for this chapter, an assessment is necessary. Your child can take the assessment in the comfort of your own home, on your own computer; just download the program onto your computer. If you prefer a test in pencil and paper mode, then print the whole assessment after you download it. The downloadable assessment is called the Learning Ability Assessment, also known as ALA-PLA.

Once the assessment is complete, the next step is to transmit records to me via e-mail (FantasticElasticBrain@gmail.com), including the paper and pencil part of the assessment for review. (There are at least two short sections in the assessment that require the use of paper and pencil.) I will then send the record on to SOI Systems for analysis and the correlating personalized CD and paper and pencil modules.

This Action Guide section, then, will involve doing actual SOI modules.

CHAPTER 7:

Brain-Changing Music

THE PRIMARY GOAL OF THE Listening Program (TLP) is to train or retrain the human ear and brain in the numerous skills that comprise auditory processing, so that listeners can process sound without distortion. When that occurs, the auditory system is in balance, and people become able to listen both to others and to themselves.

I have always used TLP or the Integrated Listening Systems (iLs), with my clients. These two high-quality programs, located in Ogden, Utah, and outside Denver, Colorado, respectively, both follow initial work done by Alfred Tomatis, an ear, nose, and throat medical doctor who lived in France and originated the idea that listening to music can actually change the brain. Dr. Tomatis explored why opera singers were harming their vocal chords and realized that their ability to hear had been compromised by damage in the middle ear. Tomatis hypothesized that vocal problems of opera singers came from auditory processing problems. His theory that "the voice does not produce what the ear does not hear" is the hallmark of his research and his method. Tomatis developed a device that uses electronic gating, bone conduction transducers, and sound filters to enhance the uppermost missing frequencies. His goal was to tonify the muscles of the middle ear. He also developed programs to improve balance, hearing, coordination, energy level, and vocalization.

In my own work with learners on what I call brain-changing music, I have them wear high-quality headsets and listen to gated music of Mozart, Haydn, and chants for thirty minutes to an hour from an iPod. Why do I think this specialized music changes brains? I, for one, experienced some unusual emotions, including aggression and anger, when listening to the language CDs in the TLP program and the auditory processing Focus Program in the iLs program. I analyzed my days when the changes took place and could find nothing unusual in my day. The only difference was that I had spent an hour with headsets on listening to Mozart or Haydn. I also had some clients, namely Jacob and Kiley, who experienced heightened emotions when first listening to the CDs or iPod. I am convinced that the music from the CD or iPod was causing the behavior changes for a day or two in each child. It is my custom in my Brain Ways office to have my clients listen to TLP or iLs while they challenge their vestibular on the walking rail and the Belgau Platform Balance Board.

Most of my clients also perform Brain Gym® or brain bag activities that cross the midline while listening to the music. For ocular-motor development, the children sometimes perform vision therapy exercises, too. I feel that performing activities while having the vestibular tuned in to the music is like getting a double dose of vestibular development.

Advanced Brain Technologies developed The Listening Program (TLP) that I used with my children when I began my work in Brain Ways. *The Listening Program Level One Kit Guidebook* contains an explanation of the function of our ears:

> Sound waves are produced by air pressure oscillations that carry language, music, and the sounds of our environ-ment to our outer ear. Once sound has reached our outer ear, it moves through the auditory canal. Sound then passes through the eardrum, middle ear, and temporal bone to reach the inner ear. The inner ear converts the mechanical

energy of sound waves into electro-chemical messages that are carried along the auditory nerve to the brain. The brain then can perceive the messages and compare them to previously stored sounds to interpret the information.

Anywhere along the auditory pathway, distortions can occur in auditory perception. These distortions can adversely impact listening and create auditory processing problems that can lead to a host of social, emotional, and academic challenges. An event as seemingly benign and treatable as a middle ear infection can cause the brain to permanently misinterpret or distort the perception of sound. These perceptual distortions not only manifest as auditory processing problems, but also create stress that is revealed in the voice, energy levels, social skills, and self-perception. (Doman 2004)

Not all of my clients have an auditory processing issue, but many have one or more symptoms of auditory processing problems, including:
- Has difficulty listening and paying attention
- Misunderstands spoken information, directions, or questions
- Frequently asks "huh?" or "what?"
- Needs to have directions or information repeated
- Has poor auditory sequential memory
- Is easily distracted by background noise
- Finds some sounds uncomfortable or painful
- Has trouble hearing similarities and differences in sounds
- Has poor phonics skills for reading

(Doman 2004)

I have not done case studies of my clients, but many case studies on the TLP and iLs websites feature children who were not making progress until someone turned on the TLP or iLs iPods; then those same children showed phenomenal changes. (See www.advancedbrain.com for TLP and www.integratedlistening.com for iLs.)

In the following pages, the reader will be able to understand even more from the exact words of the developers of Integrated Listening Systems. I hope readers will find this information as fascinating as I do. The following information about the iLs Programs comes directly from their website: www.integratedlistening.com.

> iLs programs include classical music that has been acoustically modified to provide enhanced or filtered signals in certain frequencies, as specific frequencies are believed to be correlated to certain brain functions. The music is loaded on an iPod paired with special headphones which deliver it through both air and bone conduction (a low frequency vibration that is conducted by bone to the cochlea and vestibular system). Simultaneous to the auditory component, the user engages in visual, vestibular and motor exercises which maximize the interaction of the systems outlined below.

THE SCIENCE OF HOW ILS WORKS

This is essentially a type of training: neuronal connections in these pathways are strengthened and new connections are established through repeated sessions of multi-sensory input. iLs programs are customized, i.e. individualized for each person's therapeutic goals, and they gradually become more complex and challenging as they progress.

Vestibular System

Directly connected to the cochlea of the inner ear, the vestibular system is responsible for balance, coordination, muscle tone, rhythm and awareness of the body in space. It plays a key role in organizing motor output and posture. The vestibular system, along with proprioceptive inputs, also has a strong impact on attention and emotional regulation. Once these systems are functioning well, children and adults are better able to participate in higher brain functions such as reading, writing and expressive language. iLs provides specific and comprehensive stimulation to the vestibular system through bone conduction delivered via headphones, balance board activities, and body movement exercises.

Impacted Skills: coordination, balance, focus, self-regulation

Auditory

Decoding, phonemic awareness, listening in a noisy classroom and speaking clearly require efficient processing and storage of information. iLs processes classical music to emphasize different frequencies per therapeutic objectives. The goal is to train the ear and the brain to analyze and process sound more efficiently and accurately. For example, the iLs Reading & Auditory Processing Program focuses on the mid-range frequencies of the English language to train and improve the perception and discernment of the subtle differences in closely related phonemes. This skill is essential for the development of spelling and reading proficiency. As a result of repeated listening, the vestibulo-cochlear system improves the subcortical transfer of auditory information to the brain.

Impacted Skills: pitch discrimination, auditory processing, spelling, mood, concentration, balance

Visual Motor

The subcortical visual motor system has direct neural connections to the auditory and vestibular systems. All three of these systems must work together for proper balance, coordination, reading and sound localization. iLs programs activate these systems with visual tracking and visual perception exercises; in fact, ocular motor improvement ranks as one of the consistently strongest areas of change resulting from iLs programs.

Impacted Skills: balance, coordination, reading and sound localization

Proprioceptive

By improving the sense of one's own body—where it is, how to control it, how to move it—to the point where we don't need to think about it, we are freeing up the brain to focus on higher order activities. Children and adults who improve their proprioceptive abilities are able to approach learning and communication tasks in a more relaxed and regulated manner. iLs's movement program focuses on building proprioceptive abilities with specific exercises in each session.

Impacted Skills: attention, calm, athletics, coordination, daily movement, confidence.

Parasympathetic System

The Autonomic Nervous System (ANS) controls many organs and muscles that work in an involuntary, reflexive manner. The ANS is important in two situations: emergencies that require us to "fight" or take "flight" and non-emergencies that allow us to "rest and digest." The part of the ANS which governs the latter is the Parasympathetic Nervous System (PNS). iLs's auditory program stimulates the PNS through the Vagus nerve (auricular branch). Many children and adults beginning iLs programs are in a state of hyper-arousal, not far from "fight or flight." The gentle stimulation of the PNS brings about a balance of the ANS which is reflected by increased calm and self-regulation.

Impacted Skills: behavior, ability to focus

Cerebellum

The cerebellum has 10% of the volume of the brain, but it has 50% of the brain's neurons. In computer terms, it's our processor, receiving input from sensory systems and various parts of the brain, and integrating these inputs to fine tune motor activity. Most neuroscientists agree it is involved in motor functions, cognitive functions such as attention and emotional functions such as regulating fear and pleasure responses. The iLs Playbook's repetitive activities are believed to stimulate cerebellar function. Inputs from the visual, vestibular and auditory systems, session after session, train the cerebellum to become efficient at processing multi-sensory information.

Impacted Skills: motor control, "automaticity" (motor activities becoming automatic), processing.

Hemispheric Integration

Receptors in the body deliver sensory information to the brain (and vice versa). If these receptors and the pathways leading up to the brain are not working because they were damaged or did not develop properly, the activity level of the brain decreases and different areas of the brain may not communicate with each other properly. In addition, connections between the right and left sides of the brain must be robust in order to allow for proper communication to take place between the different areas involved in higher brain function. The combination of listening and cross-lateral activities in the iLs Playbook require the almost constant transfer of information from one hemisphere to the other, "exercising" the bridge that transfers information, the corpus callosum.

Impacted Skills: processing speed, cognitive functions, emotional health

Reticular Activating System (RAS)

The Reticular Activating System (RAS) is a network of neurons deep in the brainstem that receives input from all sensory systems. It sends non-specific information to the brain to "wake it up." It is involved with regulating arousal, sleep-wake transitions, alertness, appropriate arousal to attend to the task at hand and even prepares the motor system for action. The RAS is engaged through both the auditory and movement components of iLs's multi-sensory training.

Impacted Skills: ability to attend and focus, behavior

(All of the information on pages 127–133 is available on www.integrated listening.com. Used with permission.)

CLIENT SUCCESS

I believe every child who has worked with me has benefited from the stimulation of the brain from either TLP or iLs. Some of their stories are below.

Isiah

One method I use to show growth in auditory processing skills is a pre- and post-assessment using Scan C Test for Auditory Processing Disorders in Children—Revised, created by Robert W. Keith (2000). Isiah, one of my clients, completed the Scan C assessment with me scoring Low, "Disordered," in distorted sounds. He evidenced Central Auditory Processing Disorder with his score. Isiah then did all the Brain Ways work, twice a week, including the iLs Focus Program entitled Reading and Auditory Processing. On his post-test, he improved in all areas, including those he had scored Borderline-Normal, two of which moved up in the Normal range. But his largest gain was in the distorted sounds, where he had been dysfunctional on his first test. Isiah moved up to Low Normal in that distorted words test.

Kiley

Another client, Kiley, showed similar growth. Her mother purchased the TLP program so Kiley could listen five days a week. There is an assessment in Scan C in which the child hears two different words at the same time, one in the left ear and one in the right ear. Kiley scored in the Low range, below borderline, in the left ear and right ear two-words-simultaneously assessment. She did not show a preference for right or left ear, she just could not say which word was first most of the time, and rarely knew both words. The TLP and iLs programs helped her not only in auditory processing but with her ADHD symptoms as well.

Like Kiley, not all clients have issues only with auditory processing. The Focus Programs in the Integrated Listening Systems offer four choices in the playlist to help in tandem with other brain areas:

- Sensory Motor
- Concentration and Attention
- Reading and Auditory Processing
- Optimum

Here is a useful diagram from my iLs Pactitioner Training Course Manual:

Looking at the above diagram, I can easily visualize Kiley's needs: Yes, "Sensory Processing" for her auditory processing difficulty with two words spoken simultaneously in her left and right ear. Also in the area of Regulation, Impulse Control and Emotional Regulation were huge areas of need for Kiley, who threw tantrums normally more closely associated with two-year-olds.

Although I am not an expert on these programs, I do know that the TLP and iLs perform "gating," where the highest notes and the lowest notes are in certain ranges for each separate area. I understand the notes gated for ADHD are in the lower range and provide a calming effect, which certainly helps my ADHD learners and others, like Kiley, who seem to always be in "flight or fight" mode.

Dominic

Not all of my children show difficulties in auditory processing. However, I have all my clients listen to music while they are performing activities and exercises in my office. If you look at the "Impacted Skills" listed for each system in the above paragraphs, it is apparent that the listening programs can influence a variety of behaviors. As Dominic progressed through second and third grades, he also listened to Concentration and Attention in the iLs, and he made good progress at Brain Ways. Most of my ADHD kids showed improved behavior, in fact, and the listening programs definitely get some of the credit.

Abbie

I urge those clients with sensory integration dysfunction to listen to the Sensory Motor Focus Program on their iPod five days a week. iLs has a Home Rental Program that allows children to listen at home while performing Playbook activities. Abbie, my new six-year-old client, showed marked improvement in her sensory integration from the very beginning. Her parents ordered the rental program on our first appointment. I told Abbie that listening to her music while on the balance disc as well as working on the Playbook activities would help limit the discomfort she felt from her shoes, underwear, sweaters, etc. If you were a mother of a six-year-old who cried through six pairs of shoe changes "because they itch," you would welcome the opportunity to have your child listen to music and perform activities in the hope that the shoes drama would not reoccur. In Abbie's case, she has been noticing that her sweaters and sweatshirts have not bothered her as much since beginning to listen to her music. As for underwear, she is not willing to try wearing it again—yet. However, one day she told her mom that she thought the music and exercises were making her happier.

Alex, Jacob, and Kenny

I have also worked with these "Gumby-like" boys, who could barely stand on a balance board without falling right off when they arrived at Brain Ways. Then I started them on the music while building up various vestibular-strengthening exercises. I cannot state for certain that it was the music that caused the improvement, as we complete a variety of activities in Brain Ways, but the children certainly improved their core. By the end of forty Sensory Motor iLs Focus programs, all three boys could accomplish walking rail balancing, jumping on a trampoline with rhythm, spinning on the Rotation Board, and knocking off targets while balancing on the Belgau Platform Board.

Matthew

I had worked with Matthew in eighth grade. I saw him infrequently in ninth and tenth grade—just for special situations. During eighth grade, while we focused on his organizational skills, he also listened to the entire Concentration and Attention iLs program. After his sophomore year, Matthew's parents asked what they could do to prepare him for eleventh grade, as he had not done as well as they had expected in tenth grade. My suggestion was that he complete the iLs Focus Programs throughout the summer. He listened at least an hour a day, five days a week during July and August. When junior year of high school arrived, I was no longer called for special occasions, because there were none. Matthew felt confident and his grades showed it.

Federico

I also want to tell the story of a dear elderly gentleman who was the land-lord of my office in Guatemala. When I met him, he had already suffered a number of strokes. He was no longer able to go out and about as he had been accustomed to. I suggested that he try listening to TLP "to change his brain." I did not meet with his neurologist to see if there were changes noted. I did not meet with him in my office. I simply provided my ten TLP CDs and a good headset. All I know is that after two months of daily listening an hour a day, he told me that he had driven to the bank to deposit my rent check. Again, I think it was the brain-changing music that provided him the opportunity.

Due to improvements I have witnessed in my clients' abilities, I truly believe TLP and iLs change the brain. I believe it is worth it to listen an hour a day while challenging one's vestibular, doing the Playbook, playing LEGO, crossing the midline, or any of a variety of activities. The potential for music to establish new brain connections, especially when coupled with Brain Ways activities, can be life changing.

ACTION GUIDE

You need to have a certified practitioner monitor your child's use of the Integrated Listening Systems. As I mentioned, there is now a rental system in place so that children can listen and perform the Playbook activities five days a week. You can also purchase the system from iLs, but again, you need someone to monitor the use of the system. I live in Alameda, CA and would be happy to Skype with you. I can set up Internet monitoring of your child's use of the program, where you input which sessions s/he is accomplishing.

CHAPTER 8:

Dominance Profiles

WHAT IS A DOMINANCE PROFILE? It's a learning-styles assessment system developed by Paul Dennison, PhD and Gail Hargrove Dennison designed to identify the lateral dominance of eyes, ears, and hands (and, later, feet) in relation to the dominant brain hemisphere. In her book *The Dominance Factor: How Knowing Your Dominant Eye, Ear, Brain, Hand & Foot Can Improve Your Learning*, Carla Hannaford, PhD, illuminates thirty-two different Dominance Profiles. People's individual profiles exhibit many variations. One person may have a dominant left hand but a dominant right foot. Another individual might be dominant in her left ear but have a dominant right eye. Hannaford explains all the possible variations, emphasizing that knowing one's profile can lead to better understanding and learning.

Hannaford states, "Lateral dominance is innate and influences the way that your body and mind initially process information. These innate or basal patterns are particularly useful for understanding school children. But, they also illuminate the behavior of adults in stressful circumstances" (1997, 15).

PROFILE A   Profile A
                   Hannaford, Dominance Factor, page 53

Profile A: Right ear, right eye, right hand, right foot, Left brain (the dominant parts are dark) (Hannaford 1997, 58).

Few parents have even heard of Dominance Profiles when I mention that I want to check their child's. Although I am not an expert on the profiles like Dr. Hannaford is, I have used them enough in my practice to test for dominance. These spot-on profile assessments lead to Dr. Hannaford's categorizations of how kids learn best and what helps them when under stress.

Dominance Profiles also relate well to the goals I develop for my clients. My main focus in working with children in my office has always been the integration of the left and right hemispheres of the brain. My kids perform pendulum work, brain bag activities, Brain Gym®, and listen to the Integrated Listening Systems. Nearly each item I use with learners is designed to enhance the communication between brain hemispheres.

Hannaford writes about the left brain and right brain using the terms "logic hemisphere" and "gestalt hemisphere" instead of "left" and "right" because in some instances they are transposed. I have mentioned before that the two distinct hemispheres are connected in the middle by a bundle of nerve fibers called the corpus callosum. Hannaford writes that each hemisphere develops and processes information in a specific way. The logic hemisphere (usually on the left side) deals with details, parts of the whole, processes of language, and linear analysis. By contrast, the gestalt—meaning, whole-processing or global, as compared with linear—hemisphere (usually the right side) deals with images, rhythm, emotion, and intuition. I always tell my kids we are building new neural pathways to augment the freeways running through the corpus callosum. Hannaford writes a similar metaphor:

> The corpus callosum between the hemispheres acts as a superhighway allowing quick access to both linear detail in the logic hemisphere and the overall image in the gestalt hemisphere. When there is good communication between the two halves, the result is integrated thought. The more that both hemispheres are activated by use, the more connections form across the corpus callosum. The more connections, the faster the processing between both hemispheres and the more intelligently we are able to function. (1997, 18)

Actually, it is necessary to use both hemispheres of the brain to be maximally proficient at anything. But, as noted above, we all have a degree of hemispheric dominance and in times of stress, or new learning, people will exhibit a preference for either logic or gestalt processing. (Hannaford 1997, 19)

On the next page is the table of similarities and differences of the two hemispheres for the readers who are not familiar with the terms:

Logic	Gestalt
Processes from pieces to whole	Processes from whole to pieces
Parts of language	Language comprehension
Syntax, semantics	Image, emotion, meaning
Letters, printing, spelling	Rhythm, dialect, application
Numbers	Estimation, application
Techniques (sports, music, art)	Flow and movement
Analysis, logic	Intuition, estimation
Looks for differences	Looks for similarities
Controls feelings	Free with feelings
Language oriented	Prefers drawing, manipulation
Planned, structured	Spontaneous, fluid
Sequential thinking	Simultaneous thinking
Future oriented	Now oriented
Time conscious	Less time sense
Structure oriented	People oriented

When Under Stress	When Under Stress
Tries harder, lots of effort	Loses the ability to reason well
Without results	Acts without thinking
Without comprehension	Feels overwhelmed
Without joy	Has trouble expressing
Without understanding	Cannot remember details
May appear mechanical, insensitive	May appear emotional or spaced-out

(Hannaford, Carla 1997, 20)

I want to point out that the school systems of the United States favor the logic-brained learner (Profiles A-HH). Hannaford says, "The gestalt dominant learner (Profiles I through PP) has not been as positively reinforced in our educational system" (1997, 21). Of course, brain integration is necessary for optimum, high-level learning.

I could write a proliferation of information regarding dominance and Dominance Profiles. However, I wish to continue emphasizing how important the brain is, including communication between its hemispheres and how my programs address their integration. So, rather than discussing all thirty-two of the Dominance Profiles, I will address the one that is most common in my clients: the L profile.

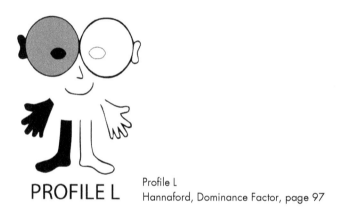

PROFILE L

Profile L
Hannaford, Dominance Factor, page 97

Profile L Rt. Brain, Rt. Eye, Rt. Ear, Rt. Hand, Rt. Foot (dark areas indicate dominance) (Hannaford 1997).

I myself fit the L profile, as do many of my clients. This profile indicates that we are right-side dominant, including right eye, right ear, right hand, right foot and right brain. The problem that can be caused by this profile is that under stress, it is hard to access the preferred brain hemisphere to receive and/or express information. Here are some characteristics that Hannaford lists for Profile L:

- Learns best through movement and by focusing on the whole picture, context, and emotional relevance to self.

- Needs to move while processing internally with minimal external sensory stimulation.
- Needs quiet time alone, especially when integrating new ideas and under stress.
- When relaxed may see, hear, and easily communicate the details and sequence of information, both verbally and written.
- Appreciates metaphors, examples, and associations when problem solving.
- Prefers not to follow step-by-step instructions. Tends to start by imagining the end results and then intuitively doing what seems appropriate.
- Movements tend to be spontaneous and fluid when relaxed. Under stress may move forward with caution, feeling clumsy and stuck.
- May have difficulty communicating, seeing, listening, and remembering when under stress. Will see the whole picture but not know where to start to chunk it down into the linear pieces of language to express it.
- At great disadvantage under stress in that they cannot access their dominant hemisphere with sensory input and are therefore totally shut off. However, when relaxed, can more easily access logic/gestalt integration than the other gestalt profiles. The dominant gestalt processing works with the preferential sensory-motor access of the hand, eye, and ear to the logic hemisphere, causing logic/gestalt processing to be more integrated.

Helps:
- Will benefit from sitting where they can process internally, quietly, and move without disturbing others.
- Activities that help: Active 8s and Thinking Caps from Brain Gym®, blinking while tracking with the eyes, megaphones, integrated cross-lateral hand and foot play like knitting, writing, and drawing with the non-dominant hand, conscious walking, dancing, soccer, and martial arts like Tai Chi.
- An integrative balance of art, music, movement and

interpersonal skills, combined with cognitive endeavors in linguistics and mathematics will be highly beneficial. (Hannaford 1997, 96–97)

When I am stressed, I remember some of the above and try to help myself. With children, we talk about how our brains work and how it is best to access the logic side with sensory input. We also discuss what happens when under stress and how to try to deal with accessing the brain hemispheres. I have talked with classroom teachers about some of my clients' profiles and what would benefit the child in the classroom. The older kids advocate for themselves, similarly to the Central Auditory Processing Disorder students.

There is one thing from the list I am reminded of whenever I work with my clients on their homework. These Profile L learners need that quiet time after a question is asked to process the answer. Sometimes they need to walk around as they process in their minds.

When I assess a new client's Dominance Profile, I show the parent and the child the list from Hannaford. We discuss what works and does not work for the child. When parents ask me about an activity or a sport that would help their child's development, I always consult the profiles to see which one will be helpful for that particular child. A child so right-dominant as Profile L might tend toward tennis or basketball, while the integrated cross-lateral hand and foot play of soccer might be more beneficial for his/her day-to-day living.

In Profile L, movements tend to be spontaneous and fluid when relaxed, but under stress may feel clumsy and stuck. I want to add—and I tell my clients this is how I feel in those health club step and dance classes—that the capacity to exhibit good technique, like a specific dance step, may deteriorate when stressed. I get so flummoxed in those classes that I am "stressed out" after the very first steps.

SUCCESS STORIES

So many kids think, *It's my fault—I'm stupid*, when they start out. Then, when we go over the list, so many kids get a *wait, it's* not *my fault!* feeling.

As they gain understanding, the self-blame rolls off their shoulders. It is not their fault that they are totally right-side dominant; it's simply how they are. Then we begin discussing ways to relieve stress. However, we also KNOW, *Oh, my hand, eye, ear, and foot are not helping me get to my brain. It's not my fault I can't do this sequence right at this moment.* This new knowledge is a relief or reprieve from the *It's my fault—I'm stupid* refrain, as the following stories attest.

Jake

Jake was a ninth grader just getting used to public high school when he first officially arrived at Brain Ways from Castro Valley, CA. His mother was concerned that he was falling behind right from the beginning of school in social studies, English, and math.

When I completed Jake's profile, he tested as Profile B. As Hannaford pointed out, the US school system tends to favor A-HH profiles, so I was not so worried about Jake at first. However, when looking at his profile, I could see why he was having trouble in the Auditory-Sequential style practiced in 75 percent of teachers' classrooms.

Three Functional items were noted under Profile B that fit Jake: Visual, Verbal, Movement. "Learns best by focusing on the visual details. Processes by analysis, verbalization, and writing," is listed first under Profile B (Hannaford 1997, 56). Jake had the ability to follow step-by-step *visual* instructions, but only his math teacher accompanied her verbal explanations with some visuals. Jake was a typical Profile B in that he needed to see or write in order to learn, and he was struggling because much of the teaching was oral lecture.

The help I gave Jake came directly from the Profile B lists of characteristics and also from the "Helps" section: "When the ear is limited during stress or with new learning, may have difficulty processing auditory input, especially details and specific information" (Hannaford 1997, 56). This fit right in with the remedy I spoke with Jake and his mom about: Jake would benefit from sitting at the front of the room on the right hand side to better access his dominant ear (Hannaford 1997, 57). Of course, like many ninth grade boys, Jake had always chosen the desk as far away from the teacher in each classroom. He had to make the change in his seating arrangement to take into account that his left ear was dominant.

I am happy to say that going over the problem he was having in the three classes was crystal clear to Jake when he saw his Profile B DomiKnow and the lists that described his challenges and what he could do about them. So, Jake advocated for himself and either changed his seat or, if there was a seating chart, explained to his teacher how we had discussed at Brain Ways that he needed to be seated in the front right. Mission accomplished, Jake started to do better in his classes.

There were other suggestions that he followed as well: Profile B people do better when they write what they hear, so Jake began writing down as much of what his teachers were saying as he could. As his auditory processing was challenged, this helped him organize for himself the lecture into an orderly visual sequence on paper. I would say Jake definitely profited in significant ways from knowing his Dominance Profile.

Abbie

Abbie is a six-year-old with Profile I. Now that I've explained some of her I traits to her parents, they have both experienced some "aha" moments about their daughter. As Abbie is still quite young, it is a bit difficult to explain to her that "when relaxed [she] may easily communicate the details and sequence of information, both verbally and written," whereas she "may have difficulty communicating under stress" (Hannaford 1997, 84). However, it has helped her parents to understand there is a reason why sometimes she seems so "able" but in another instance seems totally "un-able." Now that they know that stress is the likely culprit, they can encourage her to do Brain Gym® Hook-ups or Cross Crawls.

Because Abbie is also Sensory Integration challenged, she is not likely to do Tapping. Although we have gone over it a few times, she does not "want to tap myself when I am angry or mad," she says. She is, however, willing to do Brain Gym®, and Hannaford lists a couple of other "Helps": Activities that help cross-lateral hand and foot play, like knitting, writing and drawing with the non-dominant hand, walking, dancing, and martial arts are all activities that interest Abbie. Her parents signed her up for an acrobatics class where she is thriving. Using an integrative balance of art, music, movement, and interpersonal skills, combined with cognitive endeavors in linguistics and mathematics, will be highly beneficial, states Hannaford (1997, 85), and Abbie's parents have tried to provide that on her six-year-old level.

Also, according to Hannaford, these Profile I learners will benefit from sitting in the middle front of the room, where they can access their dominant ear and eye. This change of seating was the first thing Abbie's parents were able to do in her first grade classroom.

This Profile I's challenge may be to access the pieces of information and be able to put them together in a linear, logical manner so she can communicate. As I work more with Abbie and she matures into second grade, I am hopeful we can work on ways to do just that.

Lisa

I mentioned that most of my clients were Profile L. My daughter Lisa was one of the many: a very Gestalt (right-brained), emotional middle school girl. Earlier in this chapter I listed all the characteristics of the Profile L, so I will not repeat them all here. I want to focus on just a couple of the most important descriptions of Profile L for Lisa: Movements tend to be spontaneous and fluid when relaxed. Under stress, may move forward with caution, feeling clumsy and stuck. May have difficulty communicating, seeing, listening, and remembering when under stress. This learner will see the whole picture but not know where to start to chunk it down into the linear pieces of language to express it (Hannaford 1997, 96).

These descriptions so fit Lisa. I recalled her third-grade teacher saying that sometimes she could not understand "where Lisa was going" when she was talking. After learning of Dominance Profiles, I could see that those times, which occurred as early as age seven, were most probably related to this L Profile: all the sensory input to the brain is stymied when under stress. I remember well the day Lisa read out loud in fourth grade (for the last time) and came home still embarrassed that she'd read "burrow" as "burrito." She had been stressed about getting called on and then totally flummoxed when kids laughed.

As Lisa was my own child, I was able to do certain things that might not be available to all parents. For one, Lisa switched schools for eighth grade. The new school fit her learning style much better. She was able to move about the back of classrooms, if she felt the need, or walk to the bathroom, without the teachers admonishing her. There were many more hands-on team projects. Her delight in school lessened the amount of stress she had felt in the other school the previous two years. Her ability to communicate, listen, and remember improved dramatically just because the stress of the school situation was no longer with her daily.

I want to add that Lisa, after a dreadful ninth-grade year at a college prep–type school, found an alternative high school that fit her learning style. I was, at first, against her going to an alternative high school because of dubious reputations I had heard of in gossip sessions, but after the first few weeks I could see my daughter flourishing. The small class sizes suited her, as did the classes in cooking and gardening that were interspersed with her academic classes. She graduated as Student of the Year, selected by the teachers. As a proud parent, I'll add here that Lisa went on to graduate from San Francisco State University with a degree in business/marketing.

You can look back on the many characteristics of Profile L learners in the list in this chapter. What I have homed in on with all my clients is this: This learner is at great disadvantage under stress in that they cannot access their dominant hemisphere with sensory input and are therefore totally shut off. I show each client his/her profile, and if it is Profile L, I show on the DomiKnow how their brain is inaccessible when they are under stress. Then we work on activities to de-stress situations: deep breathing, Emotional Freedom Technique (EFT) Tapping, and Brain Gym®, especially drawing the Active 8s. Many a child has told me, "I just drew my Active 8s until I calmed down." That is the beauty of knowing one's own self, specifically one's profile type.

ACTION GUIDE

To assess your or your child's Dominance Profile and to learn ways to help yourself or your child on your own, you will need to purchase The *Dominance Factor: How Knowing Your Dominant Eye, Ear, Brain, Hand*

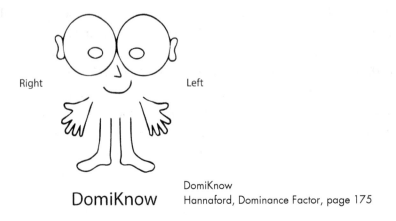

Right   Left

DomiKnow

DomiKnow
Hannaford, Dominance Factor, page 175

& Foot Can Improve Your Learning by Carla Hannaford, PhD. Each profile is listed in order and accompanied by a very easy-to-understand graphic, which Hannaford calls a DomiKnow.

Also included with each profile is an explanation of which hemisphere is dominant, as well as lists of functional strengths and limitations under stress. Hannaford includes in each profile how a learner of that type of profile learns best, what type of processing is preferred, if the profile points to the person being a visual learner or auditory learner, and a list of the challenges of the profile. In each profile is a section labeled "Helps" that lists ways in which parents can help their children with that particular profile.

CHAPTER 9:

Emotional Freedom Technique

THE BEST DESCRIPTION OF Emotional Freedom Technique (EFT) I can include comes from a compilation entitled *Freedom at Your Fingertips*: "The premise of EFT is that, unlike Western medicine's focus on our bodies as a chemical system, our bodies also have an energy system. The cause of all negative emotions is a disruption or blockage in that energy system," writes editor Ron Ball. "These blocks include fears, phobias, anger, anxiety, grief, depression, trauma, worry, guilt and other restricting emotions that also contribute to physical problems. When you clear the disruption or blockage using EFT, you have physical and emotional freedom" (Ball 2011, 1).

When I am working with my clients, there are times when they get frustrated, angry, or anxious. I know that sometimes kids get in trouble in school when they have similar emotional feelings. I like to teach them EFT to release the emotions they are feeling because it is hard to learn when the brain is blocked. It is actually hard to perform anything when the emotion is bubbling up.

EFT is a type of meridian tapping that combines ancient Chinese acupressure and modern psychology. Tapping utilizes the body's energy meridian points by stimulating them with your fingertips—literally tapping into your body's own energy and healing power. From pain relief, to healing childhood traumas, to clearing limiting financial beliefs, to weight loss, body image, and food cravings, to fears and phobias, Tapping is proving to be a powerful, well-researched technique that is easy to learn and apply. (For more information, visit www.thetappingsolution.com.)

In my office, I used the EFT Tapping procedure called the Root Cause Technique. (See this chapter's Action Guide for a description of the full procedure.) In this EFT, my clients and I use two fingers to tap on each meridian point on our face and body while also repeating a script. We repeat each of the seven taps for a series of three times, each time repeating the script. Each client is, of course, different. Some children dislike Tapping because they are overly sensitive to touch. Some children prefer to do Hook-ups to calm down. But some of my kids really mastered EFT, and it is also effective in many "shortcut" ways. I hope the reader will explore Tapping for him or herself.

CLIENT SUCCESS

Stories such as Dominic's and Matthew's, below, illustrate the power and potential for EFT to improve the quality of children's lives. With proper assessment and specific integrated approaches, they can grow and mature into productive individuals.

Dominic

My client Dominic was a seven-year-old second grader when he made his first visit to Brain Ways. For the first few months of Dominic's visits, I thought it was important for both Dominic and his mother, Catie, to do EFT. She was upset with his behavior at school, where his impulses got him into trouble. So the three of us sat together at the beginning of each of Dominic's office visits and tapped.

In my office we performed a technique in which we started with imagining spreading our roots deep into the ground, like a tree. Then, as we would tap two fingers on each of the seven meridian spots, we would state sayings related to the tree and our emotions. (See the entire exercise in this chapter's Action Guide.) It was a nice feeling at the end of each session, as each of us had said our "own thing."

EFT proved to be quite beneficial to Dominic. I listened to Catie's worries while he worked on integrating his left and right brain hemispheres on office apparati. Dominic completed the L assessment of the SOI and scored off the charts, which did not surprise us. Many ADHD children are gifted. They just have trouble slowing down enough to exhibit their talents.

In Dominic's case, he had an annoying proclivity to make odd noises in class, which distracted his classmates and aggravated his teacher. He just made noise. If you asked Dominic at the time if he were making noise, he probably would not have noticed that, indeed, he was.

Catie was willing to advocate for Dominic. She spoke to his teacher to allow him to have a lap blanket and a bungee cord attached to his desk. The cord allowed him to "play" with a movable object when needed. The blanket had weights sewn in to it that seemed to calm Dominic down.

Catie was a kindergarten teacher. Before and after school in her classroom was a perfect time for Dominic to work on brain bag activities, the Cross Crawl, the walking rail, and Active 8s. This time really assisted him in organizing his brain.

I had received small drawings of Emotional Freedom Technique (EFT) spots from Diego that were just perfect for Dominic to use to remember for Tapping. I did not know if a seven-year-old would engage in Tapping independently; however, both Dominic and his mom seemed to really need to release some emotions, especially anxiety. And, indeed, Dominic began to tap the spots from Diego's simple diagram in his schoolyard.

It was most helpful for Dominic to use the Brain Gym techniques and the EFT Tapping procedure during recess and school time when he felt he was stressed. Dominic had collected a large number of "yard duty referrals" for behavior that was not acceptable. These referrals and his subsequent punishments diminished as he used EFT instead of "exploding" and getting into trouble.

Neither adults nor children have to go through the entire process of The Root Cause Technique. There are many shorter variations on Tapping that can be successful. Dominic, for example, could envision the chart and tap on some spots with the intention of "cooling down," and that would save him from a referral.

I learned from Dominic that seven-year-olds could understand when they were under stress and do something about it. This would help me with other children who were one-side dominant and had trouble accessing their brain.

Matthew

I write about Matthew and our concentrated work on his executive skills. Matthew's own work is also mentioned in this book's ADHD chapter. In addition, Matthew used Emotional Freedom Techniques (EFT) when he felt himself under stress. (Please note: I am talking about a teenager here.) Matthew was willing to tap his forehead, temples, under his eyes, above and below his lips, under his armpit, and lower on his chest. He did this in front of his high school office staff. The reason that he was willing to tap was that it worked.

Matthew told me the story of how he had written and printed on his computer an English paper that was due. The next morning, when he reached in his backpack to turn in the paper, it was not there. He told me, "The whole time I was calling my mom to bring my paper to school, I was tapping, Betsy." This was in a busy high school office! I think the story shows how useful it was to Matthew when he was feeling stressed.

He was also a learner who regularly employed Hook-ups, the Brain Gym® calmer-downer, when he felt the need. His high school was a private Catholic college prep, so there were plenty of days when Matthew felt overwhelmed enough to use Tapping or Hook-ups.

ACTION GUIDE

This chapter section entails you and your child completing three cycles of a Tapping routine to release emotions, clearing you/your child's energetic pathways throughout the body for better brain processing and learning. As I have mentioned, there are many versions and many shortcuts. You can use the diagram at the beginning of this chapter and just repeat how you want to feel, like "I am calm."

On the next page, I am including the Root Cause Technique, which is the EFT sequence with words that Dominic, Catie, and I used at the beginning of many of Dominic's sessions. I sincerely hope you will work with it to gain emotional release when needed.

Root Cause Technique

Even though I _____I choose_____.

1. **Eyebrow:** I am eliminating all the sadness in the deepest root causes of this_____.

2. **Under eye:** I am eliminating all the fear to the deepest root causes of this _____.

3. **Little finger (near nail):** I am eliminating all the anger to the deepest root causes of this_____.

4. **Eyebrow (opposite):** I am eliminating all emotional trauma to the deepest root causes of this_____.

5. **Under mouth:** I am eliminating all the shame to the deepest root cause of this _____.

6. **Top of head:** I am eliminating all the guilt to the deepest root causes of this _____.

7. **Heart:** I am eliminating all the grief to the deepest root causes of this _____.

8. **Index finger (near nail):** I forgive myself for ever taking this on. I don't need this _____any longer, because I am now able to replace it with _____.

CHAPTER 10:

Dyslexia and Dysgraphia

THE DICTIONARY DEFINES DYSLEXIA as follows: "any of various reading disorders associated with impairment of the ability to interpret spatial relationships or to integrate auditory and visual information" (dictionary.com). Dysgraphia is a form of dyslexia where the difficulty is primarily with handwriting. People with dysgraphia have problems with legible penmanship (Davis 1997, 250).

Children and adults with dyslexia usually have healthy eyes and sharp eyesight. However, a substantial number of individuals with dyslexia have other visual problems. Depending on its severity, a learning-related vision problem can sometimes be misidentified as dyslexia because there are similarities between them. However, it is more common that children with dyslexia also have a visual component that is contributing to their difficulties.

When a child struggles with reading and learning, it is important to first rule out the possibility of a vision problem. If a vision problem exists, treatment may involve glasses, optometric vision therapy, or both. Optometric vision therapy treats vision problems that can interfere with learning to read or reading to learn. Once the vision problem is treated successfully, tutoring and other special services can become more effective.

I am not a scientist, but Carla Hannaford is, and she writes in *Smart Moves*:

> Dyslexia has been considered a visual problem because it shows up and by definition is associated with reading difficulties. Interestingly, the central deficit with dyslexia, which is universal in all languages, is related to the metalinguistic ability to decompose words into sounds, link the sounds (phonemes) to symbols and to make these skills automatic. The development of that phonemic understanding is thought to begin in utero, possibly as early as 9 weeks, as the semicircular canals develop and the embryo responds to sound with movement. At that time the Moro reflex develops which allows the embryo/fetus/child to respond to danger with a protective action. If there is much maternal stress, the fetus will often be in the Moro reflex and the other reflexes important for vestibular development will be delayed. Without this development, the fetus and child will have difficulty hearing the patterns of language, the phonemes, and later linking them to symbols to read. (1995, 170–71)

Reading this, I thought about how the vestibular system played a big part in dyslexia and how what we were doing in Brain Ways every session was helping develop the vestibular system. I knew I was checking for retained reflexes so I could work on those that were retained. I also looked for ways to work with the young learners coming to me who were already feeling "defeated" by schoolwork. I wanted to find a method of correction for dyslexia that was not tedious to the child or adult, and worked. And I found it.

Some of my learners came to me with a diagnosis from an educational psychologist stating "dyslexia." When this happened, I would ask myself, "Did this person find ways to assist him?" I would look over all the paperwork, including the traditional ed psych evaluations of the WISC and the Woodcock, and see numbers that indicated the child was not up to grade level. In some cases, such as Ricardo's, a vision problem was

what had been causing so many problems for him in school and in doing homework. For Diego, who had never been diagnosed with dyslexia, I did the dyslexia protocol with him because of his dysgraphia. For others, like Meches, Olivia, Miguel, Esteban, and Andre, who did the disorientation protocol and successfully placed their mind's eye in a location spot behind their head, some did all the Davis Symbol Mastery list and some did not. It is rather like my own little scientific study: Do the Mastery list, start happily reading. Don't do the List and stay with your problem.

To give you a clue to one of the main reasons I like Ron Davis's work, all that need be said is he calls his work *The Gift of Dyslexia*. You are welcome to read his book and go over all of his thought processes in coming up with his theories and corrections. In this book, however, I am just going to tell you about disorientation, the mind's eye and the Davis Symbol Mastery. Because this book is to help you help your child or yourself, I write about what I do—and what I do is help my kids with the Mastery list. This is a quote from Davis: "When someone masters something, it becomes a part of that person. It becomes part of the individual's thought and creative process. It adds the quality of its essence to all subsequent thought and creativity of the individual" (Davis 1997, 113).

According to Davis, disorientation is a common occurrence. It probably happens to you, the reader, sometimes. I know the feeling of disorientation when I am in a car and a nearby car moves, giving me the feeling that I am the one moving. Disorientation also occurs when we are overwhelmed by stimuli or thought. It occurs when the brain receives conflicting information from different senses. During disorientation, your brain might see things moving that really are not, or your body may feel as if it is moving though it is not. The senses are altered.

With dyslexia, disorientation probably happens more often, because a person with dyslexia can cause it to occur without realizing it. Davis says dyslexics use disorientation on an unconscious level in order to perceive multi-dimensionally. Until beginning school or trying to learn to read, the child with dyslexia uses disorientation to resolve confusion. This works when dealing with real physical objects but causes disorientation when a confusing symbol is encountered. Take a look at the child with a view of the word "CAT" from top, back, side—all points of view. (See illustration on the next page.)

Davis writes of the symptoms of disorientation, saying a person's perceptions become distorted. The main senses that become distorted are vision, hearing, balance, movement, and time. Interestingly to me, his lists of symptoms could be the list to send a child to vision or speech therapy, or to label a child ADD or ADHD. He then adds four abilities that only those with dyslexia evidence:

- The ability to intentionally access the brain's perception-distortion function.
- The ability to consciously view mental images three-dimensionally and move around them in mental space.

CATTACIAOCAT
OATTACIAOOAT
CAIIAOTAOCAT
ACTTOAIOAACI
ACTTOAACIIOA
AOTTCAAOIICA
ATCOTAAICOIA
CTAATOCIAAIO
ATCOIAAICOTA
ATOCTAAIOCIA

(Davis, 1994, 84)

- The ability to experience self-created mental images as real-world phenomena; in other words, being able to experience imagination as reality.
- A tendency or preference to think nonverbally by using pictures of concepts and ideas, with little or no internal monologue. (Davis 1997,125–126)

In referring to the mind's eye, Davis writes, "It is important to note that in the Davis procedures, one does not see, look at or sense anything in, through, or at the mind's eye. One sees or looks *with, from* or *out* of the mind's eye." (1997, 128) When you are looking at something, you have to be looking from somewhere. When you see something in your imagination, you are looking *from* or *out* of your mind's eye.

According to Davis, the mind's eye does not have a location but a multitude of possible locations. It is wherever the owner perceives it to be. He talks about disorientation, such as when people with dyslexia look at an alphabet letter and within a second they see dozens of different views of the letter—from the top, the sides, and the back—which disorients them. "In other words, the mind's eye is mentally circling around the letter as though it were an object in three-dimensional space. It's like a helicopter buzzing around, doing surveillance on a building" (1997, 129).

I use the Davis Perceptual Ability Assessment to determine if my client has the ability to move the mind's eye around easily to see a mental image from different perspectives in space. I work with my learners as Davis suggests, establishing a location for their mind's eye for the express purpose of reading so that they no longer hover like a drone or helicopter, perceiving words from all different angles. Then I teach the person how to control the position of the mind's eye and move it to the optimal viewpoint for reading.

After Orientation Counseling, where we set the location for the mind's eye for reading, we move on to basic Symbol Mastery. This is another of Ron Davis's steps. Symbol Mastery is used to master the alphabet and punctuation symbols so the learner is no longer triggered into disorientation when they see a letter, numeral, or punctuation mark. The child creates each symbol in modeling clay, identifies it, and learns its use. The idea is to master the symbol so there is no more disorientation.

I always do some extra activities just to reinforce the letters of the alphabet so there will be no confusion when we get to words. We play games like, "What's the letter before 'r'?" We also look for letters in newspapers, magazines, and books. We talk about font and notice different typesets for certain letters like "a" and "ɑ" . We also do some writing of letters in handwriting work.

My clients work with and master punctuation marks as well—first in clay, then looking for printed ones, then finding the definitions and usage in grammar books. Punctuation marks can be just as disorienting as letters and words if they are not mastered.

Then we do a bit of spell reading, just to be sure the learner's brain and eyes scan from left to right while reading. In spell-reading, the child or learner just says the letters in order. I say the word; the learner repeats the word. It is not phonics; it is just practicing left-to-right eye movement.

Then we have fun with Symbol Mastery for Words, my favorite part of working with kids with dyslexia. A lot of adults and children "over-concentrate," and that is not the key to Symbol Mastery for Words. Instead, we research the words, play with the clay, and have fun. It is playful but also a huge learning experience. Depending on the age of my

client, I require different things, but usually that includes a definition—
or three—of a word. Did you know the word "so" has seventeen definitions in a dictionary?

Miguel was a freshman in high school. He had a Mac Airbook, so he
wanted to do all of his work on that. We compromised such that he could
look up definitions and cut and paste them into his Mac, but he still had
to make the word and image in clay.

I often have my kids write a sentence to show me they know how to
use the word, like the example of the word "in" by Katelynn here:

After they do the work with a word, they truly have mastered it. Almost all of my learners like making the 3-D clay model of the concept. When parents are willing to take over the helper part of Symbol Mastery for Words, I use today's technology and have the learners take pictures on their cell phones so I can see they have the word, the 3-D sculpture, and either a sentence or definitions.

CLIENT SUCCESS

The success these children have after going through the processes mentioned is really gratifying to see, as often they had never before picked up a book to read for enjoyment. Afterward, all of them began to read!

Andre

Andre was practicing moving his mind's-eye location with me. He was standing on one foot with his eyes closed and I asked him to move his mind's eye to the clock on the wall. He literally fell over to his right. He enjoyed the experience so much he wanted me to direct him to put his mind's eye in other places in my office to see if it could make him fall over again. We had fun, and he totally understood when I told him the location for his mind's eye for reading was *fijo* (set) in the location we had established.

Meches

Meches was relatively defeated when she came to my office for the first time because she had just flunked fourth grade. I told her that her dyslexia was a gift and showed her the title of Ron Davis's book, *The Gift of Dyslexia,* but she was not exactly feeling "the gift" just yet. She took the CR SOI assessment with me and tested in the "Gifted" stanine in a number of aptitudes, one of which was creativity. I remember when we were about halfway through the Davis Mastery list, she looked up from one of her very creative 3-D constructions of clay and said, "If I'm so smart, why do I have to keep coming to your office?" My answer was that she had not finished the list with her mom and needed to do all the words to make reading easier. She completed her words and went on successfully in school.

Diego

Diego started at Brain Ways when he was twelve years old. In the German-Guatemalan school system, that was fifth grade. On a Thursday, Diego's mother interacted with his English teacher after school. Frau D. told her that Diego was sure to get an "A" on the test the following day, as they had just had a review and Diego knew every answer. On Friday, however, Diego came home with his test with a grade of 40 percent. Diego and his parents were devastated. Diego was in fear of flunking the entire year of fifth grade if he flunked this one class: English.

The following week, Diego and I began our work together at Brain Ways. His mother lamented that his handwriting was so bad that teachers could not read whether he knew the answers on tests or not. Therefore, Diego started at Brain Ways with a diagnosis of "dysgraphia."

Diego will always be one of my favorite clients. Of all the children who have come through Brain Ways's door, Diego is the one and only one for whom my cat, Say Whoop—who typically ran and hid when anyone under five feet tall came through the door—would come running and plop right in front of him. Diego called him "my buddy," though with his German-Guatemalan English accent it always sounded like "my body."

Ronald Davis lists seven reasons for dysgraphia (2003, 67). I reviewed those seven reasons with Diego's mom, and explained to her that I was leaning toward treatment for Diego's possible dyslexia as a means to treat his dysgraphia.

I began the protocol immediately. It entailed placing a location behind the head to locate the mind's eye and then, once Diego was comfortable using the spot, moving on to clay or Play-Doh to roll out punctuation marks and the 242 words listed by Ron Davis.

Diego had no problem quickly imagining a slice of pie in his hand. He willingly let me locate a place for his mind's eye, anchored by his ears, behind his head. He followed directions well and was a willing participant. Soon, Diego and I were making 3-D clay figures and words from the Davis Mastery list.

This became a marvelous experience, as Diego had a great imagination and a good memory. Soon, we transferred the responsibility of the word list to home, and Diego continued to make four words in clay each day. His mother was a wonderful aide, drawing a little picture of his 3-D figure, as well as the word in Spanish and German. Each time Diego arrived at Brain Ways, I would quiz him on the 3-D picture he had in his mind of the words he had finished. He progressed through all of the 242 words!

Diego would also bring vocabulary words, spelling words, and grammar exercises to his Brain Ways sessions. We started conjugating English verbs while hitting the Pendulum Ball from the Belgau Platform Board—"eat, ate, have eaten; write, wrote, have written; go, went, have gone . . ." Diego practiced whatever was critical in school while hitting the Pendulum Ball at the targets, sometimes with the Vestibular Motor Control Stick (VMCS) and sometimes batting with his hand, wrist, or elbow. His grades improved.

We also worked on handwriting within and outside his schoolwork. The German-Guatemalan boy did not want to write in the American alphabet style, but his writing was much easier to read when he did. There are certain letters in German cursive that are nearly identical, adding to his illegibility.

Ultimately, all of Diego's hard work paid off: he passed English! When he passed fifth grade, his parents took him out to dinner to celebrate.

An additional breakthrough happened, when, about a month later, Diego, with his mom keeping track, finished his Mastery list of clay figures and words.

We celebrated the end of the clay-making in a Brain Ways fashion with Nutella crepes, but Diego also celebrated by picking up the first Harry Potter book in the series,

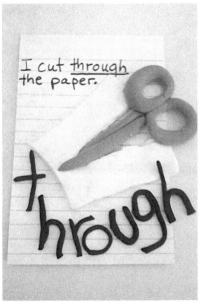

which his mom had read to him, and read it to himself! That breakthrough led to Diego reading EVERY Harry Potter book in the series . . . all within the next five months! The boy who did not like to read, who had never picked up a book "just for fun," all of a sudden found he COULD read easily and quickly.

Another of Diego's difficulties, indicated by the Scan-C Test for Auditory Processing in Children, Revised, was that he had difficulty processing what he was hearing in his right ear if he was simultaneously hearing "anything" in his left ear. At his school, the Director did not want to provide any concessions or "free passes" to Diego because of this problem, so I enlisted Diego's help. As I had previously worked with a child at Brain Ways with the same problem, I knew I needed to put Diego in charge. He was to be sure that when the teacher was speaking, he would have his right ear "turned on" and his left ear "turned off." As sixth grade began, Diego positioned himself in a desk at the back of the room, with no one and no noise to his left. His problem, that year, was solved by the makeup of his classroom's seating chart. By the time he advanced to classes where he moved around to different rooms, Diego had two advantages in regards to his Competing Words and Sentences differential: he understood that he would have trouble processing on the right if there was sound going into his left, and he knew where to position himself. With intentional seating and nearly a year's worth of listening to The Listening Program at Brain Ways, his auditory processing had improved.

In follow-up talks I conducted with his parents, Diego's mother, Karin, expressed that she had felt so guilty throughout his schooling. She was always scolding him about not doing his homework, not trying, not studying. In sixth grade, when it was obvious that Diego had made such great strides, Karin wrote a letter to her son and placed it on his bed. In the letter, she wrote how sorry she was for thinking he was lazy. When teachers had complained to her about his homework or poor performance, she had felt bad and took it out on him. Karin expressed how much she loved Diego and that her reprimands had been made out of love. Diego never mentioned the letter to his mom until a couple of years later. He told her that whenever he perceived things to be "bad" or "going wrong" he would read her letter, feel her love, and regain his strength.

Diego's dad laughingly shared an incident that occurred the year after Diego passed that fateful fifth-grade year. Diego expressed to him, "Last year you were always complaining to me about my schoolwork and reprimanding me, but this year you aren't." His dad was laughing because Diego did not find school so difficult once he finished the 242-word Mastery list. Karin confirmed that she never had to nag or scold Diego about schoolwork again—ever since the sixth grade.

Diego continued to work with me on Structure of Intellect (SOI) modules, improving many of his underlying aptitudes. I cannot count the large amount of SOI modules Diego accomplished with me. But I can tell you that, as of this book's printing and eight years after Diego's sessions full of aptitude building, he is a successful engineering student at a university in Germany.

Miguel

Miguel was a fifteen-year-old high school freshman when he came to Brain Ways. As he had previously been diagnosed with dyslexia, we started and accomplished all the activities, including the mind's eye placement activities, for helping those with dyslexia. We also did Vickie's protocol for midline processing, which I have found can have a profound impact on ADHD-labeled kids, of which Miguel was one. In all the activities, Miguel was a willing, eager participant.

When we talked about the prescription for completing the 242-word Mastery list, Miguel immediately went into "time-saving" or "energy-saving" mode. Miguel suggested alternatives to my usual requirements. We finally agreed that if he would take a cell phone picture of his 3-D model of the word and spell it out with Play-Doh, then he could use his computer to present the word and the definition or sentence.

Using each word in a sentence was optional as long as Miguel gave at least three definitions. He worked well this way, always bringing his folder full of words he had conquered, sometimes bringing his computer, if the printouts were not handy. It is no small task to look up the definitions. Try it yourself. Look up the word "as" and count how many definitions there are for that little two-letter word. I think you will be surprised.

While Miguel was working with me in Brain Ways, he was attending a school that had been losing its students. Miguel's class was down to five. Being the fun-loving, social kid he was, he really wanted a bigger school for high school. So we worked an extra session per week for the weeks leading up to his entrance examination.

I remember teaching Miguel some of the eye movements from NLP/ Neuro Linguistic Programming. He tried hard to remember that he was to look up to the left to access his memory when taking the entrance exam. His mother and I both laughed as he looked up to his right when I asked him what he was going to do the following morning in the exam; the kid with the high creativity was telling us he was going to access his creativity and solve the problems on the exam using that part of his brain. Whatever eye movements he actually used during the test, I do not know. What I do know is that Miguel passed the exam and started his sophomore year in September.

His mother reported that teachers in Miguel's previous school had often complained about his low abilities in this or that, but the new school never made any complaints or sent notices to her about his academics. She worried that maybe the standards of the new school were not high enough; I prefer to believe that Miguel changed his brain to work better in Brain Ways.

When Miguel was finishing up with the words on the Mastery list, we started reading both silently and aloud during our sessions. He had always been afraid to be called on to read out loud in school because he thought that the other students would laugh at him. I explained that reading aloud involved additional processes in the brain, his Brain Ways had improved his processes, and he would be better able to read aloud now. He also understood that he could now read silently much more efficiently, as he had made pictures in his mind for all the little words that used to tie him up when he was reading.

I doubt it will surprise the reader to know that Miguel began to read on his own, and continues now to read voraciously. His big breakthrough, according to his mom, came when he volunteered to write and read a speech at his high school graduation. She reported that she was nervous sitting in the audience, thinking how painful it had always been for him to read aloud, but Miguel read his speech to applause from the audience. It was a breakthrough for him.

In 2016, seven years later, Miguel has a good job in Madrid, having successfully graduated from a well-respected hotel and restaurant management school in Spain.

ACTION GUIDE

Buy the books *The Gift of Dyslexia* and *The Gift of Learning*, both by Ronald D. Davis. Follow Davis's very complete instructions on how to deal with disorientation, setting a location for the mind's eye, and completing the Mastery list of 242 Words. The goal is to make reading a good experience that your child will relish. You will do this with your child—and your child will find reading so easy that s/he will want to read!

CHAPTER 11:

Attention Deficit (Hyperactivity) Disorder

MANY LEARNERS HAVE ENTERED my office with an ADD diagnosis. Generally, the child has been diagnosed before his/her parent seeks my help. There is a long list of target symptoms that imply ADD or ADHD, including the following:

- easy distractibility
- inability to stay focused
- impulsivity
- poor attention
- difficulty sustaining attention
- low frustration tolerance
- angry outbursts
- mood swings
- difficulty with organization
- chronic procrastination

- difficulty prioritizing
- a tendency to worry rather than act
- a subjective inner feeling of noise or chaos
- a tendency to hop from topic to topic or project to project (Hallowell and Ratey 1995, 236)

I have assisted children who showed many of the symptoms in the list above but whose parents did not want to put them on medication. I have also worked with learners who were taking Ritalin, Concerta, Intuniv, or some other stimulant. I have provided services for adults with ADHD. I have firsthand experience with this condition because I was diagnosed with ADHD myself when I turned fifty years old. As is often the case, parent and child are alike; my daughter also fit most of the criteria on the list above. After my diagnosis, I read every book and article I could find about ADD and ADHD. Then I started my personal pursuit of what to do about being a person with ADHD, including deciding whether I wanted to be medicated.

For an extensive discussion regarding whether or not to treat ADD/ADHD with medication, I reference Drs. Hallowell and Ratey. These two foremost ADD authorities will provide readers with a variety of pros and cons (1995, 236–38).

As I read and researched and learned, I became more and more secure in the idea that brain integration was the way to go. I decided against medication for my child and me. I not only read many books, I also attended workshops on The Learning Breakthrough Program with Dr. Frank Belgau, Brain Gym®, and retained primitive and postural reflexes. Throughout this book I discuss a variety of activities I do with my learners to help integrate the left and right hemispheres of their brains. This integration, I feel, is the number one aid to those of us with ADHD. I believe that when the brain is integrated, ADD individuals have a better chance at controlling impulses, thinking before interrupting others, stopping themselves from those "Chatty Kathy" times when the motor-mouth runs, and tempering many other ADHD symptoms.

My learners are also always involved each session with the Integrated Listening Systems playlist for Concentration and Attention, which I

believe gives the kids a double dose of vestibular challenge as they perform their activities. This makes the neural pathways that are being formed by crossing left to right and vice versa stronger. My clients spend time on the Belgau Boards, hitting a Pendulum Ball in a left-right sequence, or on the Rotation Board, spinning left-right. Learners that work with me are expected to complete their Brain Gym® and brain bag exercises every day at home, and they work on them when they are with me in the office. With the younger set I use Brendan O'Hara's CDs with a variety of songs/ activities that help them cross their midline, the imaginary line in their head that separates and left and right hemispheres. With young children it is easier to explain passing an object in front of their nose or belly button, or otherwise using their hands to cross from left to right and vice versa, than to call it crossing the "midline."

In addition to all the activities my ADHD clients perform, I introduce organizational tools that can help ADD individuals. Some years ago, when I hired an ADHD coach for myself, she entered my home and made me remove all the papers I thought were "in neat piles," such as newspapers, magazines, mail, letters, notes, every used envelope, etc.

Frances also believed in using one planner for everything, and she ordered me to buy an expensive Franklin Covey planner.

I whined, thinking of many planners I had purchased and never really used. "But I will just lose it," I complained.

"Nope," Frances said, "you won't lose it, because you will commit to this planner and you will keep it by your side at all times."

Sure enough, I never misplaced or lost my Covey planner, just as Frances predicted.

Any or all items on the following list can help ADD individuals if they attend to the tools (as I did with the Covey planner) that they have chosen for self-organization from the following options:

- lists
- reminders
- notepads
- appointment books
- filing systems
- Rolodexes
- bulletin boards
- schedules
- In and Out boxes
- answering machines
- computer systems
- alarm clocks and timers (Hallowell and Ratey, 1995)

Of course, almost all of the above items can be programmed into one's smartphone today. I know individuals who have systems for answering their voice mails only once a day. They throw their snail mail in the recycle bin or garbage before they bring anything unnecessary into the house. Other folks have bulletin boards that look like personal maps. I personally set alarms and timers throughout the day, and I encourage my ADHD adult clients to do the same. I give my iPhone "personal assistant," Siri, reminders for later in the day and week; she always answers, "OK, I'll remind you," and sure enough, my phone dings in at the scheduled time with "Call Susan" or "I have a workout appointment at the gym."

Anything that can be part of a regular schedule—week in, week out—is a plus for anyone with ADD. Swimming lessons on Tuesdays, Ms. Betsy on Thursday, and game night with parents on Friday are examples of a regular schedule for my students. For older children and adults, the calendar on a smartphone can also provide a structure, with reminders, that can lead to being more on task and on time, and ultimately to feel better about themselves as they actually accomplish "life."

For my clients who do not use smartphones, I still prefer a big clock with two magnets that ADD kids can move around the rim. It is more visual for them than setting an alarm on a phone. I have my learners put a magnet on the time they are starting a section of homework, with another magnet at an end time a short time away. The kids then decide what chunk of their homework they can accomplish in that time frame. This automatically creates checkpoints throughout their homework. Quite a few students felt their homework "went faster" as they worked with the clocks-with-magnets.

EXECUTIVE SKILLS

What are "executive skills?" Sometimes people think I am talking about an executive of a company, like the CEO. No, the "executive" comes from the word "execute"— as in, "executing tasks." I could write a book on developing executive skills, but a good one has already been written by Peg Dawson, EdD and Richard Guare, PhD called *Smart but Scattered: The Revolutionary "Executive Skills" Approach to Helping Kids Reach Their Potential*. In it, the authors provide the following list of executive skills:

- Getting organized
- Planning
- Initiating work
- Staying on task
- Controlling impulses
- Regulating emotions
- Being adaptable and resilient (Dawson and Guare 2009, vi)

Because the prefrontal cortex is not fully developed until age twenty-seven, executive skills that are undeveloped in adolescence can cause many a headache for parents and contribute to low grades in high school, especially if turning in homework is still a problem. For many middle school students, especially those with ADHD, the brain-based skills become more important and more critical as learners venture into the world with decreasing parental supervision and guidance. Ultimately, of course, they are essential to successful management of adult life. Middle school is the time in which the lack of executive skills becomes very noticeable, as parents' direct supervision is reducing then.

ADD individuals in particular tend to lack executive skills; however, as the *Smart but Scattered* authors note, these skills *can* be improved if they are taught directly. When a teenager begins to grasp and gain control over his/her executive functions, that is when s/he has a structure that truly assists with ADHD characteristics.

ADD/ADHD & VISION

Undetected and untreated vision problems can elicit some of the very same signs and symptoms that are commonly attributed to ADHD, including impulsivity, hyperactivity, and distractibility. Due to these similarities, some children with vision problems are mislabeled as having ADHD (Granet et al. 2005, 163).

A 2005 study by researchers at the Children's Eye Center, University of San Diego, uncovered a relationship between a common vision disorder, convergence insufficiency, and ADHD. The study "showed that children with convergence insufficiency are three times as likely to be diagnosed with ADHD than children without the disorder."

Dr. Granet of the Children's Eye Center commented:

> We don't know if convergence insufficiency makes ADHD worse or if convergence insufficiency is misdiagnosed as ADHD. What we do know is that more research must be done on this subject and that patients diagnosed with ADHD should also be evaluated for convergence insufficiency and treated accordingly. (2005, 64)

Vision problems can have a huge impact on academic performance and behavior in the classroom. Even if a parent does not suspect a vision problem, my feeling is it is worth it to be sure by arranging for a comprehensive vision examination with a qualified COVD optometrist. Why should a child experience learning or behavior issues and be labeled ADHD when visual skills deficiencies may be the culprit? Please refer to the Action Guides in Chapters 3, 4, and 5 for activities that improve visual skills.

CLIENT SUCCESS

I have found my ADD clients to be some of the most creative and fun kids to work with. It is a challenge having ADHD, but many kids have made great strides in "taming" their ADD proclivities through our work together.

Catherine

Catherine was a sixth grader with combined ADD-ADHD. She was also my first client who had almost perfect balance — a well-developed vestibular. She had other deficits for us to improve, but she could close her eyes, stand on one foot, and count forever without falling. You might think you can do that, too, so go ahead. Set the book down and try standing on one leg with your eyes closed without *any* movement of your body. Isn't as easy as it sounds, is it?

Catherine needed Emotional Freedom Techniques (EFT) as well as left-right hemispheres brain integration for her ADHD. She needed to tap her two fingers on the meridian spots. She was not a willing participant in this. We came up with a compromise. She could hold Say Whoop, my cat, in her lap and tap using the other hand. I say this was a compromise because Say Whoop was not a willing participant either, but that is what worked.

I met with a number of Catherine's teachers at her school to provide them some Brain Gym® activities that they could have her perform to integrate her two brain hemispheres. I stressed that it might be nice for them to include the entire class in performing the exercise, so that Catherine did not feel singled out. Imagine my surprise when I heard that after a math teacher introduced the Active 8s to her class, having her students make an infinity sign in the air with their thumbs, Catherine raised her hand and volunteered to teach the Cross Crawl. This would also help her classmates with brain integration.

Matthew

Matthew came to Brain Ways about a month into eighth grade. According to his mother and grandmother, his ADHD was off the charts and they worried he was never going to make it through eighth grade. With me, Matthew engaged in all of the Brain Ways regimens: took the SOI assessment and completed many modules, worked on the Belgau platform board with the pendulum, listened to the iLs focus program for Concentration and Attention, worked on his handwriting, sometimes brought homework to do, and did many of the Brain Gym® exercises both in my office and daily at home. All of our activities integrated his right and left hemispheres, making it easier to learn, as well as helping him control his ADHD symptoms.

Matthew did a school project concerning the medication dilemma during his eighth-grade year. His thesis question was, "Do you believe that ADHD children should be medicated?" He was very interested in finding out who thought what and why. He, himself, remembered being unable to sit still in kindergarten and first grade. He was thirteen years old at the time he reminisced about the first days of second grade after his doctor and his parents had agreed to try Concerta. He remembers being amazed that he was actually able to sit in a chair.

As part of his project, Matthew interviewed a PhD doctor in the M.I.N.D. clinic at the University of California, Davis. Ultimately, although Matthew's research resulted in ten people who favored providing medicine for ADD/ADHD and ten people who were against giving a stimulant, he remained committed to his path. Matthew and his family could always tell if he forgot a medication dose on any given day. I recall him as a junior in high school laughingly telling me about an ADD friend who had for the first time been prescribed an ADHD medicine. The friend was so amazed at all he was hearing and learning in class as compared to before medication treatment. Matthew just chuckled and said, "I told you so."

Most of my meetings with Matthew were focused on improving his executive skills. He and I would decide on the specific executive skill we were going to work on. We would first discuss why it was important. Then we would list ways to practice each skill. We would often develop a checklist for him to review each night at home. I would try to enlist his parents in assisting with the skill we were focusing on each week. Every time we met, we would go over Matthew's progress. Sometimes he would need more than two or three weeks to further develop the skill. None of it was easy for him, but with attention to "writing the date on every paper" or "turning in homework" or "setting your backpack by the garage door each night after the checklist," we progressed. As the months passed, we kept practicing the previous executive skills we had worked on while also focusing on new skills.

When Matthew's eighth-grade year was drawing to a close, I received an invitation to his eighth-grade graduation, along with a couple of after-parties. His mom and dad stated he never would have passed eighth grade without "Ms. Betsy." I was honored! Matthew really made great strides with his executive skills. The brain integration we practiced all year made a big difference regarding his ADHD behaviors as well.

Sebastian

Sebastian was a third grader at the German School in Guatemala. He evidenced ADHD, or maybe he was just the most curious child in my office, but he could not walk in without going and touching at least three things before he started his session. He had an incredible knack for finding something either out of place or new and would pick it up, play with it, ask about it, or otherwise engage in off-task behavior to start each session. If I had a notebook with a new client's name on it, Sebastian would head right for it and ask me about that new child. If a pencil sharpener, the level for the balance board, or the sand minute "hourglass" was in reach, it would be in Sebastian's hands.

Sebastian was also one of my hardest workers. When one is working one-on-one with a child, one does not see the same ADHD behaviors kids display in the classroom. In Sebastian's case, he was a willing learner and did his daily exercises like clockwork, so his ADHD traits lessened over the course of the year and a half I worked with him.

Isiah

Isiah was being home-schooled in the sixth grade when he first attended sessions at Brain Ways. Isiah had been diagnosed with ADHD while quite young. Two of the reasons his mother mentioned for taking him out of a traditional public school was his distractibility and inability to sit quietly and listen to the teacher. Isiah was able to attend Brain Ways twice a week and we were able to accomplish much in the way of right-left brain hemisphere integration, an entire series of Concentration and Attention of the iLs Playbook, and many SOI modules.

Isiah's first love in life was basketball, so it was easy to devise dribbling drills using both the left side of the body and the right hand and vice-versa. He did not have a basketball hoop in my office in which to practice shooting, but he assured me he practiced left-handed lay-ups and other drills using his non-dominant hand.

The lessening of typical ADHD behaviors is relative, so it is hard to say emphatically that Isiah's work on the balance boards, knocking off targets, and all his left-right work was the cause of his ability to now sit in a normal classroom; regardless, he was better able to withstand public school life when he returned to the classroom about a quarter of the way through seventh grade. He decided he wanted to play for a middle school basketball team, so he asked his parents to enroll him in his neighborhood school, where, in addition to making the varsity basketball team, he did well academically, particularly in math. He was not labeled lazy or distracted, being able to control his ADHD behaviors with his left-right motor movements. In 2016, Isiah received scholarship offers from prestigious private Catholic high schools in the San Francisco Bay Area.

ACTION GUIDE

For all ages, I suggest a daily regimen like the one I wrote of in Chapter 1. Every person in the world, but especially ADHD children, can benefit from Water, Oxygen (Brain Buttons, Thinking Caps, or Energy/Lion's Yawn), Cross Crawl, and Hook-ups/PACE.

Please refer to other chapters' action guides for left-right integration movements to practice, as that is the work of the ADD person: work the traversing of the brain's pathways so that the impulses of ADHD are slowed down or eliminated.

As ADHD can be hereditary, I also want to mention an excellent book for adults that is already in workbook form. Obviously, too, the late teen or the twenty-something could also benefit from following the workbook. It follows along the principles of Alcoholics Anonymous, Overeaters Anonymous, and the other "Anonymous" groups. Fittingly, it is called *The Twelve Steps: A Key to Living with Attention Deficit Disorder*. The workbook within can really help a person struggling with ADHD symptoms. I hope the reader will take a look to see if it is a good complement for you to performing the left-right brain exercises listed throughout these chapters.

CHAPTER 12:

Sensory Integration Dysfunction

SENSORY INTEGRATION DYSFUNCTION (SID)—also known by other names, including sensory processing disorder—is a neurological disorder that expresses itself by a child being overly responsive or under responsive to stimulation from the environment. Sensory integration involves taking in information through the senses and organizing and integrating this information in the brain. If the child has a dysfunction, it is that inability to process information received through the senses. It involves all the senses, including touch, sight, smell, auditory, taste, vestibular sense of movement, and proprioception, which is the sense of one's own body position and its parts in space. When any part of this system is overly or under-responsive we call it sensory integration dysfunction. It can be just one of the senses or in multiple senses. It often affects posture and gait.

SID has many looks, so it is sometimes hard to diagnose. Children who do not seem to notice pain are under-responsive. Other times it is very clear, such as in children who cannot stand to wear socks or shoes, insisting on going barefoot or fighting each sock and shoe they try on. There are many children (and adults) who are label-phobic and cannot stand the feel of a label in their clothes. Now many labels are embedded in the garment with a printing process, helping those with the label problem. Children who cannot stand the touch of a waistband will not wear pants, underwear, or outerwear. Some girls have been known to wear only loose dresses or overalls so that nothing is "squeezing" them. This can sometimes show up in school classrooms, as when children who are extra sensitive to touch are knocked off task if their back touches the back of their chair. Many times it is the teacher who instigates off behavior when they insist that children sit up straight in their chairs! For this reason, also, SID is frequently mis-diagnosed as ADHD and children are treated with stimulants, which can exacerbate their sensory integration issues.

SID often also coexists with allergies. The child may suffer from allergic reactions to foods, dust, pollen, grass, fur, or medicines. Jacob's parents requested allergy testing when he was a toddler, so they knew already about allergies triggering some of Jacob's sensory integration issues. Crav-ings often point precisely to what is aggravating the disorders, so children who insist on certain foods or drinks might be indicating an actual allergy.

The Out of Sync Child: Recognizing and Coping with Sensory Integration Dysfunction, by Carol Stock Kranow-itz, MA, and *Raising a Sensory Smart Child*, by Lindsey Biel, are two excellent resources for parents who suspect their child may have SID: "Medicine can help the child with ADD, but medicine does not make SI Dysfunction go away. Activities that strengthen basic sensory and motor skills help the child with SI Dysfunction" (Kranowitz 2005, 20).

LABELING LEARNING DISABILITIES

The Individuals with Disabilities Education Act (IDEA) defines a learning disability as "a disorder in one or more of the basic psychological processes involved in understanding or in using language, spoken or written, which may manifest itself in an imperfect ability to listen, speak, read, write, spell, or do mathematical calculations." According to this definition, sensory integration dysfunction is not a learning disability. However, it can lead to learning disabilities when it affects the child's auditory-language skills, visual-spatial skills, and ability to process and sequence information. The child may have difficulty processing what he hears. This problem is common if he has vestibular dysfunction, because the auditory and vestibular systems are closely linked.

The child may have problems with listening skills, auditory perception, and/or language processing. He may seem noncompliant or may not follow directions well, because he cannot decode what was said.

Children with attention deficit/hyperactivity disorder (ADHD) tend to be non-sequential thinkers, sometimes with visual-spatial strengths. They share many of the symptoms of children with central auditory processing disorder and sensory integration dysfunction, and some are dyslexic (Silverman 2002, 168).

If a child has a set of symptoms that cause frustration and can be helped with some kind of therapy, you need to label the weakness so you can get the child needed services. Second, the way schools currently work, unless there's a formal diagnosis, it's unlikely that there will be any modification (which places the blame outside the child), and children are likely to blame themselves for not succeeding in school.

The problem of labeling gets intensified when you start applying multiple labels to the same human being. "Apparently our left-hemispheric labeling system can only deal with one name at a time. The notion that a child can be both GIFTED and LEARNING DISABLED sounds ridiculous to some people" (Hannaford 1997, 208).

There are two basic misunderstandings here: that the learning disabled aren't smart and that giftedness means high achievement. If someone thinks learning disabled means "dumb" and gifted means "smart," they'll think you can't be learning disabled and gifted at the same time. However, federal and state definitions of learning disabilities specifically limit the term "learning disabled" to children of at least average intelligence. So you have to be smart to be learning disabled (Silverman 2002, 166–167).

CLIENT SUCCESS

Several of my clients are challenged by sensory integration dysfunction. Their stories appear below.

Jacob

Jacob was five and a half when I met him. He definitely had sensory integration issues. I mentioned in the Brain Gym® chapter, how Jacob did not like touching his knees doing the Cross Crawl. Worse, he was growing up in Guatemala, where it is expected that a child hug or kiss each person when entering and leaving a room of adults. It was hard for Jacob to even submit to hugging his parents and grandparents. Also when I first started working with him, Jacob had no sense of where his body was in space (known as proprioception), nor a mental picture of his own body parts' interrelatedness. In addition, having sensory integration dysfunction made it difficult to work on his spatial awareness.

His successes were many in the two years we worked together. Jacob still did not relish hugging, but we had his relatives apply more pressure in their hugs and that worked with Jacob. The child who could not run and kick a ball at the same time finally was able to kick the ball playing kickball, although soccer is still not a sport he is comfortable with. His anger outbursts—at the chair, for example, if he fell off a chair—all subsided. He came a long way, as mentioned earlier, in his proprioception and integrating his retained reflexes, so Jacob was a success. He also excelled in school.

Derek

Derek was eight the day he "melted in his chair" when he heard a fire engine siren whizzing by the window. That caving in of his chest and his total discomfort was as indicative of central auditory processing disorder as the Scan C, Auditory Processing Test for Children he later took. This test, published by Pearson, confirmed that if Derek heard any noise in his right ear, he could not process what he was hearing in his left ear.

To help explain Derek's sensory integration dysfunction success, I emphasized the quote from above: "Activities that strengthen basic sensory and motor skills help the child with SI Dysfunction" (Kranowitz 2005, 20). I urged Derek's mother to insist that he do the exercises I had assigned. I had asked Derek to roll on a swimming noodle each morning for two minutes to move some fluid from his spine up into his brain. I insisted that he perform the Active 8 on the wall at least forty times as well as complete five minutes of Cross Crawling. I pleaded with his mom to not leave it up to him, or let it slide. Perhaps his next teacher would like to incorporate Brain Gym® exercises for her entire class?

Derek used the The Listening Program (TLP) throughout the summer to help with his auditory processing, but was unable to continue with me the following school year because his dad lost his job. His mother stated she was able to talk with his teacher about speaking to Derek's right side, which helped him process auditory information better. The mother reported the third grade class was much quieter than Derek's class the year before, so she was hopeful for her son.

His success came with a change in his seating arrangement when he started third grade. Knowing that the teacher or speakers needed to speak to his right ear made a huge difference in his ability to process oral instructions and lessons.

Abbie

Six-year-old Abbie's parents thought occupational therapy might help with her sensory issues. The first time Abbie came to the office, she and her mother had started fighting about her wearing a jacket when they left home, a fight that had continued in the car. When she walked in, she took the jacket off. In addition, when Abbie had just begun first grade, she cried the entire time she tried on and rejected seven pairs of shoes, exasperating her mother, who was trying to take her to school on time. She also regularly whined or screamed that underwear and/or outerwear itched too much to wear.

Abbie tended to blame herself for her inability to wear clothes and shoes. I wished she could at least relieve herself of the blame. Children who work themselves into a tizzy trying to find a comfortable feel with shoes or socks are not crying "wolf." They cannot stand to walk in the shoes or socks.

Now, as Abbie and I have worked together, Abbie has been impressed at how "things that used to bother me a whole lot" do not now bother her, such as the itchy jacket she wore her first day to Brain Ways. Her mother reported that on their way home after performing brain integration exercises with me that first day, all of a sudden Abbie asked, "Hey, what happened in there? My jacket does not itch anymore."

I wrote earlier in the book about Abbie and her changes. Abbie's parents rented an iLs music system with a Playbook, which Abbie listened to four or five days a week. She was not bothered by the headphones, which I thought would be a major hurdle. After about three weeks of doing the activities and listening to the music, Abbie told her mother that she thought the music was making her happier. I call that progress.

Another huge improvement has been in the social realm. At the beginning of first grade, Abbie was ostracized and had very few friends. This was rather devastating when other kids were making play dates and Abbie had none. Now as the integration using all of Brendan O'Hara's CDs, brain bags, Active 8s, PACE, and the Integrated Listening Systems have all kicked into her system, Abbie is changing. Now she can wear clothing that once totally annoyed her. She even admits to wearing underwear with stitching, labels, or elastic now without any problems. But the best part, in her mom's view, is that she now has friends in her class and in other first-grade classes, such that she receives play date invites and has friends accepting her invitations, too.

Iggy

All of my clients with SID experienced some level of sleep problems, but Iggy was a distinct case. Because he came to me with an ADHD diagnosis, I did Vickie's Midline Processing Protocol with Iggy. His mother called to say that for the following two weeks, Iggy, who had sleepwalked nightly since he was a toddler, had NOT sleepwalked any night. She was so relieved and happy. She wanted to schedule another protocol if the sleepwalking returned, which it eventually did. So, we did the protocol again and Iggy gave his parents two more weeks of restful sleep. His parents reported six months later that Iggy's sleepwalking had lessened over time.

ACTION GUIDE

Theoretically, this entire book could be an action guide for sensory integration dysfunction kids. Parents and teachers sometimes have to make adjustments to some of the exercises and activities, because many children with sensory issues do not like touch on the skin or to hear music when they are performing activities. However, I truly believe that if SID children cross that midline and do this book's exercises, their sensory issues will lessen if not totally dissipate.

Perform:

- Brain Gym® (see Chapter 1 and its Action Guide)
- Retained reflexes exercises and actions (see Chapter 2 and its Action Guide)
- Integrated Listening Systems (iLs) while actively engaged in Playbook activities.

More activities to integrate the left and right hemispheres of the brain, which help desensitize the overly sensitive areas, include:

Water Play. Fill up the sink or washtub with unbreakable plastic utensils, add soap, and let the child play in the water. Eggbeaters and sponges were favorite toys in kindergarten.

Writing in shaving cream. Another staple of kindergarten is writing letters and drawing on a surface with shaving cream or suds. The idea is for the child to feel.

Finger painting. This is a great activity for the senses if the child is willing. (Many SID kids find it very difficult to put that first finger in the paint, so be patient and don't force.) Once the child has been successful in moving his hands through the paint, one can add other textures, such as sand, to the paint for even more sensory stimulation.

Sand play. Few SID children will choose to play in a sandbox or walk barefoot at the beach, but if you introduce sand in a small box or a sand table they might take the first step. In my kindergarten (before I studied SID) there were students who did not like sand table "work." I would then hide small plastic dinosaurs in the sand and ask the kids to find all of them.

Play house or with a costume box. Children with sensitivities need the experiences of dress-up clothes. Having boas and scarves touch their skin helps in the long run. Wearing hats and accoutrements for different uniforms is a good sensory integration experience.

Letters on the back or hand. If your child has learned the numerals and letters, writing them on the back or on the hand as a guessing game will help with desensitizing those areas. Parents and other kids will have to feel how much pressure to place when writing, as often a soft touch will be objected to by the SID child, but a deeper, firmer pressure may work fine.

Feely box or bag. Basically cut a hole in a small box where the child can put his/her hand in the box without seeing the contents. Or use a bag. Again, this was a staple at the kindergarten stations during the Senses science unit to "study" the sense of touch. Place small objects in the box that a child can name by touching them without seeing them. The child names the object and then pulls it out for visual verification. Can use different shapes if child knows hexagon, rectangle, etc.

Many daily activities in the home can be incorporated to provide more sensory stimulation for your child. Many SID children will not undertake sensory integration activities on their own. (Think of the child who gleefully stomps through puddles vs. the child who won't enter.) Invite your child's help for home activities:

- Cooking and baking: mixing dough; feeling dough; making cookie dough into balls
- Massaging kale with olive oil
- Mixing salad ingredients together
- Caring for pets
- Using empty boxes creatively
- Gardening

CHAPTER 13:

Autism

AUTISM SPECTRUM DISORDER (ASD) is a group of developmental disabilities that can cause significant social, communication, and behavioral challenges. ASD is a very complex and complicated condition that has various degrees of characterizations, including difficulties in social interaction, verbal and nonverbal communication, and repetitive behaviors. These symptoms must have been present early in life and must still be impairing current functioning. There is a very wide range of symptoms, skill deficits, and levels of social or occupational impairment that an individual within the autism spectrum can demonstrate. The psychological guidelines include different levels of ASD, based on the amount of support the individual requires (Coulter 2009, 164).

If you suspect that your child is on the autism spectrum, it is important to talk with your child's health care provider about using the diagnostic criteria for 299.00 (autistic disorder) in the *Diagnostic and Statistical Manual of Mental Disorders*, Fifth Edition (DSM-5) for a proper diagnosis, so your child can receive services as early as possible. Also your local school systems and early intervention programs offer free evaluations, as well as provide services.

In addition to explaining what autism is, I want to say a bit at the beginning of this chapter about what autism *isn't*. Autism isn't one-word-fits-all. If you saw the movie *Rain Man* and think of all autistic individuals

as savants, you would be wrong. If you saw a child who could barely function and consider all autistic people to be nonfunctioning, you would be
wrong. It does not depend on whom you met or saw before in life, it mat-
ters who the individual is, as ASD is a huge spectrum and one word really
does not describe all. In fact, even those who have been labeled as having
autism cannot agree: some prefer to be called "autistic," while others want
only to be known as "a person who has autism."

A blog post on the College of Optometrists in Vision Development's
website (www.covd.org), printed during Autism Awareness Month and
written by Drs. Sarah Lane and Michael Cron, offered an interesting
analogy about an omelet and autism. If someone asks what you are having for breakfast and you answer, "An omelet," your response is akin to
finding out someone is labeled "autistic." There are many possibilities of
combinations of ingredients that could be included in your omelet, just
as there are many varieties of autism. To get a more precise picture of
one's breakfast, more details are required. To know more about an autistic individual, one has to meet the person, because not all people with
autism are the same.

Drs. Lane and Cron continue:

> So too it is for autism, for autism has been known for some
> time to not be a singular entity but a constellation of symp-
> toms and behaviors that constitute what is the autistic spec-
> trum. One must recognize the diversity that has become the
> Autism Spectrum Disorders (ASD). When one encounters
> an individual who has been identified as being ASD all gen-
> eralizations must be put aside and the emphasis must be on
> getting to know the individual involved. So, when encoun-
> tering an individual who has been identified as being "autis-
> tic," please realize that you need to know much more about
> that person before you can have a realistic picture of their
> capabilities and their challenges. . . . Much more informa-
> tion can be gathered on-line, including the CDC site—www.
> cdc.gov/ncbddd/autism. (Lane and Cron 2016)

Drs. Lane and Cron add, "The more we learn about autism, we discover that drastic improvements can be made with appropriate interventions and recovery is possible in some cases" (2016).

ASD Treatment

Both websites and books on autism offer strategies for treating ASD. Websites offer the reader more up-to-the-minute news and treatments than books can. My theory with websites is that the best you can do for your child is try some of the activities that you read about. If it works and you see changes, then continue the activity and discuss the results with the specialist in charge of your child. Up-to-date websites provide a plethora of insights into ASD. I have included a list in the Resources section at the end of this chapter. Books on autism, though sometimes dated, can also be helpful.

Indeed, many services in use in the treatment of ASD have been around for years. Some, like Applied Behavior Analysis (ABA) have scientific studies to back up results. As mentioned, ASD is very complex. Perhaps that is why there are so many treatments offered, including the following, available since 2005 for ASD: Activity Schedules, Applied Behavior Analysis (ABA), Acupuncture and Acupressure, Antifungal Treatment, Assistive Technology, Auditory Integration Training (AIT), Canine Companion, Cranial-sacral Therapy (CST), The Denver Model, Dietary Intervention, Discrete Trial Training (DTT), Energetic Therapies, Facilitated Communication (FC), Fast Forward, The HANDLE Institute, Hippotherapy (horse), Hyperbaric-Oxygen Therapy (HBOT), Immunotherapy, Integrated Play Therapy, LADDERS, Linwood Method, Medications, The Miller Method, Music Therapy, Neurofeedback, Occupational Therapy (OT), Picture Exchange Communication Systems (PECS), Physical Therapy, SAMONAS, SCERTS, Speech and Language Therapy, Tomatis Method, TEACCH, and Vision Therapy.

To read the entire list of treatments, refer to *The Autism Sourcebook: Everything You Need to Know About Diagnosis, Treatment, Coping, and Healing*, by Karen Siff Exkorn (2005).

I use a program similar to three of the above-mentioned ones: Music Therapy, Tomatis, and SAMONAS. I provide Integrated Listening Systems (iLs) to my clients in Brain Ways. Chapter 7 is about the changes clients have experienced with what I call brain-changing music. Also, both TLP and iLs have case studies of children with autism making gains in social skills, communication, and behavior (see www.advancedbrain.com or www.integratedlistening.com for more information on these studies).

Another very important part of helping kids with autism is checking for retained primitive and postural reflexes, as I wrote about in Chapter 2. Infants must use their reflexes to survive. To that end, if a baby is not able to show his reflex or is older than when a reflex should have been inhibited, it can be a sign of possible autism. Older children who have never had their reflexes checked also need to be screened. Sometimes inhibiting a retained reflex can open the person up to abilities that the retained reflex had been stopping. I always assess new clients. We also often perform the activities from Brendan O'Hara's Movement & Learning CDs.

Vision therapy (VT) exercises are important for many children with autism. You will learn more in the Client Success section of this chapter. Many autistic individuals have been helped by having prisms in their glasses. Any parent reading this who has not had an evaluation of their child's functional skills by a College of Vision Development (COVD) optometrist should run, not walk, to that appointment. Very young children cannot explain what they do not see, as they think what they do see is normal for everyone.

If the child has a vision problem, prisms may be just the right thing. To see what yoked prisms look like and to get an understanding of the four (base) ways in which the yoked prisms can be set and how they work to expand the eyes' views, watch this "Yoked Prism Glasses Work" at FantasticElasticBrain.com/videos. Another video, "RAD Prism Glasses" explains a bit about prisms embedded into glasses and can also be found on FantasticElasticBrain.com/videos.

Many autistic individuals have visual sensitivities or difficulties; the following descriptions are from www.covd.org.

VISUAL PROBLEMS AND AUTISM

Individuals with autism often have vision problems. Visual symptoms of autism can include lack of eye contact, staring at spinning objects or light, fleeting peripheral glances, side viewing, and difficulty attending visually.

Autistic people often use visual information inefficiently. They have problems coordinating their central and peripheral vision. For example, when asked to follow an object with their eyes, they usually do not look directly at the object. Instead, they will scan or look off to the side of the object. Autistic individuals might also have difficulty maintaining visual attention. Eye movement disorders and crossed eyes are common in the autistic spectrum (Coulter 2009, 171).

POOR INTEGRATION OF CENTRAL AND PERIPHERAL VISION

Autistic individuals can also ignore peripheral vision and remain fixated on a central point of focus for excessive periods of time. Poor integration of central and peripheral vision can lead to difficulties in processing and integrating visual information in autistic individuals. Motor, cognitive, speech, and perceptual abilities can also be affected when visual processing is interrupted.

HYPERSENSITIVE TOUCH AND VISION

Many people with autism are tactually or visually defensive. Tactually defensive people are easily overstimulated by input through touch. They are always moving and wiggling. They avoid contact with specific textures. Visually defensive persons avoid contact with specific visual input and might have hypersensitive vision. They have difficulty with visually "holding still" and frequently rely on a constant scanning of visual information in an attempt to gain meaning.

VISION EXAMS FOR AUTISTIC PATIENTS

Methods for evaluating the vision of people with autism will vary depending on individual levels of emotional and physical development. Testing is often done while the patient is asked to perform specific activities while wearing special lenses. For example, observations of the patient's postural adaptations and compensations will be made as he or she sits, walks, stands, catches and throws a ball, etc. Such tests help to determine how the autistic person is seeing and how he or she can be helped.

TREATMENT OF VISUAL PROBLEMS ASSOCIATED WITH AUTISM

Depending on the results of testing, lenses to compensate for nearsightedness, farsightedness, and astigmatism (with or without prism) may be prescribed. Vision therapy activities can be used to stimulate general visual arousal, eye movements, and the central visual system. The goals of treatment may be to help the autistic patient organize visual space and gain peripheral stability so that he or she can better attend to and appreciate central vision and gain more efficient eye coordination and visual information processing. Many COVD doctors are experienced in examining and treating autistic people as well as other developmentally delayed or nonverbal individuals (www.covd.org).

CLIENT SUCCESS

As mentioned above, I think many of my programs work for the ASD child; however, I do not have extensive experience working with ASD children because most are working with a specialist. In fact, the first success story below is not about a client of mine but about a girl who I want to include because her story tells what can and did happen with undiagnosed vision difficulties.

Rickie

Rickie's amazing story, *Rickie* (1990), was written by her father, Frederic Flach, MD, and includes some excerpts written by her. Rickie had been in and out of mental institutions for over ten years, but no one had made the link between her low visual skills and her mental diagnosis. She had tunnel vision; her world consisted of only a tiny bit of what normal eyes see. She was functionally blind, probably since she was three years old or younger. When she was three, instead of seeing an entire forest of trees when looking out a window with her father, she had been terrified, as she saw the same trees coming straight at her through the window. As those types of visual experiences continued, it was no wonder people thought she was crazy. School challenged her visual system to overload, so she had terrible anxiety about going. She did not know that how she was seeing the world was not like everyone sees the world. Objects in the distance would disappear and then she would use extensive energy trying to bring one thing into focus.

When Rickie was in her twenties, she was finally properly diagnosed and outfitted with yoked prisms, base down, by Dr. Melvin Kaplan in his Tarrytown clinic. As Dr. Kaplan explained to Rickie and her father, she could retrain her brain by wearing the yoked prisms for a number of weeks and the brain would take over and she would then be able to see without the prisms. Rickie subsequently went to vision therapy with Dr. Kaplan for six months to a year to improve her functional vision skills.

I tell you this story because yoked prisms have opened up the world for some autistic children, yet many parents do not know of the success stories with prisms. As I cannot provide a video of Rickie beginning her work with prisms, I offer you this YouTube video, which shows the difference yoked prisms make when an eight-year-old girl is reading: FantasticElasticBrain .com/videos.

In addition to doing vision therapy, Rickie practiced megavitamin therapy and other therapies in order to become a functioning person in society. She married. She studied nursing and became a nurse practitioner. Rickie lived and raised three children in Florida with her husband.

Alberto

In an older version of the DSM, my client Alberto received an Asperger's diagnosis. Now, with the DSM-5 he is labeled as ASD. Of course, as was mentioned at the beginning of this chapter, it is necessary to know each person as an individual. I tend to look at him as any other fifth-grade client who is easily frustrated, notwithstanding his label. We work on his SOI modules both on paper and on a computer. He performs many balance/vestibular activities and crosses the midline with brain bags or by firing the Pendulum Ball at the targets. Alberto also works on vision skills, not only with the Gemstone program and aperture rule but also doing VT exercises in the office and at home. Alberto listens to iLs, walks the walking rail, and otherwise does everything a fifth grader would do in my office. We have added on the EFT Tapping because he often arrives with pent-up frustration from school. The Brain Gym® exercises also help to disperse his anxious feelings.

Alberto has various retained reflexes, which we are still working on inhibiting. The retained root, suck reflex was fun to inhibit because Alberto's mouth would twitch or he would move it, so, in order to integrate it, one of the best methods is to repeat the brushing of the cheeks and chin toward the mouth. He was determined to check this one off the list and did not mind the brushing. There are others he is hesitant to work on at home, so he does not maintain a practice schedule for the Starfish or Angels in the Snow (see Chapter 2 Action Guide). He performs them in the office. But his Moro reflex is a stubborn one and will take more work. When he gets that, I am hopeful the others will fall in line.

I wrote of the Integrated Listening Systems (iLs) in Chapter 7. All of my clients listen to the music when working with me in my office; some listen at home on a rented or purchased iLs player as well. Those who work the program at home also perform the iLs Playbook activities. Alberto's parents purchased Sensory Motor iPod music with the Playbook. Alberto tries to use it daily when he vacations for six weeks in Italy with his grandparents and family. When he is with me, he only likes to listen to the Gregorian Chants on his iLs program, so I select those out from the playlists. The chants are very calming, without the need for the tactile stimulation of EFT.

A most common lack in children labeled with Asperger's is lack of gaze control. Every week, Alberto attends Brain Ways, where we work on maintaining his gaze on a pointer tip as I move it horizontally in front of his eyes. When I first met him, Alberto would be looking off in the distance yet answer, "Yes," if I asked if he were looking at the point. His eye movements were very jumpy, rather than smooth. After six months, Alberto's ability to watch the point improved dramatically. He could not always hold the gaze on the point, but intermittently he held that tip much better and longer than he had when we began. This improvement in gaze will help his reading speed. The Developmental Eye Movement Test (DEM) showed growth from the 15th percentile to the 99th percentile within his first year working at Brain Ways.

Alberto has also started working diligently on the Gemstone Foundation's Dynamic Vision Training. He is making strides in most areas, with the convergence program at this point being the only program where he remains on level one. At the time of this writing, we are working with the aperture rule (See Chapter 3 Action Guide) to also help him learn to use his two eyes binocularly.

Guy

Here I want to present a bit of the case study from the Integrated Listening Systems (iLs) website on a nine-year-old boy who was diagnosed as ASD at age three. At the time of the study, he was nine years old and was working with Debo'rah Merritt, PhD, LPC, who had an ABA postgraduate certificate and had been doing the ABA program with Guy for about a year. In the case study, you can read of all the measurements and surveys and how she measured the changes. The purpose of the study was to determine whether the Integrated Listening Systems (iLs) would complement the ABA program to a statistically significant degree. I would say it was a success.

Under the heading "Presenting Problems" were listed these behaviors of the young boy:

- Self-injurious behavior and daily aggression toward others
- Tactile hypersensitivity; he screamed when touched
- Refusal to engage others unless he knew them well; he was unresponsive to his parents' and teacher's attempts to discipline; reacting instead by screaming, lashing out physically at self or others
- Expressive language limited to one to three word statements to communicate basic needs; not reciprocal
- Play was immature and little imaginative play was present
- A one-on-one aide at school was required; in a special education classroom throughout the day

It was decided that Guy would listen to sixty sessions of the iLs Sensory Motor program while in his ABA therapy, for three one-hour sessions per week. The iLs Playbook (balance and visual exercise) were used every session. In the study, you can read further about the processes and the measurements: http://integratedlistening.com/autism-case-study-2.

What grabbed me were the results recorded one month after the completion of the sixty iLs listening and Playbook sessions:

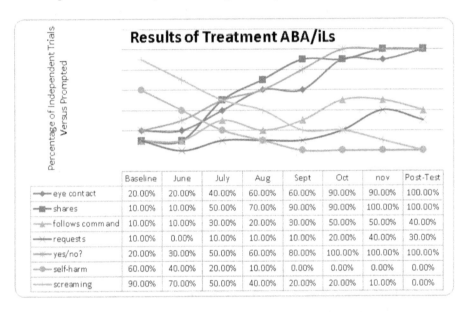

Results of Treatment ABA/iLs

	Baseline	June	July	Aug	Sept	Oct	nov	Post-Test
eye contact	20.00%	20.00%	40.00%	60.00%	60.00%	90.00%	90.00%	100.00%
shares	10.00%	10.00%	50.00%	70.00%	90.00%	90.00%	100.00%	100.00%
follows command	10.00%	10.00%	30.00%	20.00%	30.00%	50.00%	50.00%	40.00%
requests	10.00%	0.00%	10.00%	10.00%	10.00%	20.00%	40.00%	30.00%
yes/no?	20.00%	30.00%	50.00%	60.00%	80.00%	100.00%	100.00%	100.00%
self-harm	60.00%	40.00%	20.00%	10.00%	0.00%	0.00%	0.00%	0.00%
screaming	90.00%	70.00%	50.00%	40.00%	20.00%	20.00%	10.00%	0.00%

This graph shows some exceptional changes in his behavior. Just seeing the changes from 20 percent to 100 percent in eye contact, shares, and yes/no questions made me appreciate the growth. However, seeing the self-harm and screaming go from 60–90 percent of the time down to 0 percent was amazing. Having been a teacher for years and having dealt with screaming students during that time, I know getting down to zero must have relieved not only his teachers but also the other students and especially his parents and family. I can imagine how much more learning can now go forward for this little boy.

I share this story because I believe it is important for parents of children with autism to know the power of the Integrated Listening Systems and how iLS can complement the program their child's specialist is using.

ACTION GUIDE

Without doing an assessment for retained primitive and postural reflexes, we cannot identify which ones are retained, so the first thing to do is to have your child assessed and then do whatever is prescribed for inhibiting the retained reflexes. (See, for example, the Starfish and Angels in the Snow exercises in the Chapter 2 Action Guide.) However, I believe Brendan O'Hara taught his actions for integrating reflexes throughout Australia kindergartens in the hopes of reaching some children that might never be assessed. I believe all parents of preschool and kindergarten age children would benefit their child by purchasing and then practicing the songs and activities on the original CDs. Now, in the United States, many teachers trained by Brendan use the CDs in their classrooms, again blanketing all the children to reach the ones in need. Besides, they are all fun to complete. So, my next suggestion for an activity would be to perform as many of the songs, chants, and brain bag activities on Brendan's CDs. (Products available at http://movementandlearning.bigcartel.com/products.)

In my opinion, all children, including ASD children, benefit from right hemisphere–left hemisphere brain integration (see Chapter 1 Action Guide), so performing as many Brain Gym® exercises as possible is optimal.

As mentioned in the chapter, many ASD children benefit from prisms and vision therapy (VT). Please see a COVD optometrist. A good VT program may assign in-home visual skills activities to practice. In addition, there are lists of games and activities to help develop visual skills listed in the Chapter 3 and 4 Action Guides.

I also firmly believe that the iLs Sensory Motor Program aids the autistic individual in organizing the brain. (See the Chapter 7 Action Guide for information on obtaining an iLs program.)

ADDITIONAL AUTISM RESOURCES

Asperger's

The website www.aspergerexperts.com offers help from a perspective of the Asperger's child or adult because the two men who are the "experts" in the website name were diagnosed with Asperger's themselves. The website describes firsthand experience to parents who are facing a new diagnosis or already traveling the road of raising their child.

Case Studies
www.advancedbrain.com
www.cdc.gov/ncbddd/autism/index.html
www.integratedlistening.com

General Information
www.autism-resources.com
www.autism-society.org
www.autismspeaks.org
www.nationalautismassociation.org

CLIENT SPOTLIGHT:

Alex and ACC

ALEX HAS AGENESIS OF THE corpus callosum (ACC). This means Alex was born without a corpus callosum, so all those dendrites that are connecting in your brain as you read this, going from the right hemisphere (which is seeing the print on this page) to the left hemisphere (where what the right side "sees" is being interpreted and understood) and vice versa, are nonexistent in Alex's brain. Therefore, when he was developing in the womb, absolutely no dendrites traversed from left to right or right to left. Alex has no dendrites aiding in the communication between hemispheres that the rest of us rely on. Making training even more difficult, most of my work "calming" the hyperactivity of the ADHD brain (Alex was previously diagnosed as ADHD) is predicated on integrating the left and right hemispheres.

In Brain Gym®, I am always stressing "crossing the midline," integrating the left and right sides of the brain using the right and left sides of the body. I use the Active 8 as if God invented it just so my kids would integrate their rights and lefts. The Chinese have recognized the infinity sign's worth in mind-body-spirit for more centuries than other civilizations have existed. Then, along came Alex . . . who copies my lying-down ∞ as if it is standing up as straight as a first-grade teacher's 8. Without a second look, the boy sees and writes "8."

At our first meetings, his parents told me of their concerns: attention and focus, short attention span, easily frustrated, coordination, strength of core, rhythm, difficulty with transitions, and handwriting. Alex does not follow conventions in writing, leaving paragraphs of illegible writing with no spacing between words. He also has had a tremor since birth that sometimes causes such shaking that he simply cannot write properly.

I am still working with Alex, so there are many gains yet to be made. There are many neural pathways to open, many synapses to jump, and billions of neurons just waiting to be activated in his brain. Amazingly, though, he has already accomplished so much in these first months!

When he first arrived at Brain Ways, Alex would matter-of-factly tell me, "I have agenesis of the corpus callosum," as if it were an excuse for not doing something I had asked him to do with the Pendulum Ball. And I would just as smugly tell him, "No problem, kid, we are going to make NEW connections in your brain from your cerebellum in the back to the prefrontal cortex in the front . . . we are going to activate so many neurons on the way that both the left side of your brain and the right side of your brain are going to be soooo big they won't miss talking to each other, because they'll be able to take care of everything on their own."

After about the fourth time with me, Alex quit reminding me that he had ACC.

For the first couple of sessions, I did my usual assessments, beginning by checking his eyes to see if they appeared to be teaming. I also assessed his processing, crawling, creeping, balance, primitive and postural reflexes, visual skills (via the www.eyesinconflict.com online assessment), and handwriting (SOI). Then we started many of the Brain Ways activities, developing a routine for him.

I chose to begin with at least a half-hour of The Listening Program's "Classic with Nature" CDs. No matter which movements we were doing, Alex was also listening. He always attended on a twice-a-week, Tuesday–Thursday schedule. As his parents stated, Alex does not do well with changes in his schedule, but he eventually knew Tuesday and Thursday were his Brain Ways days. Then I took the Integrated Listening Systems (iLs) course, and switched him to the Sensory Motor Program on iLs, with bone conduction. (Note: Both TLP and iLs, I think, are excellent

programs for changing the brain. However, as I had from Day 1 incorporated movement with the music in my office, I felt the iLs program coincided more with my goals.) Both programs offer a bone conduction component, which means the student is receiving the benefit of the music in his/her brain via air conduction, i.e., hearing the music through the ears, as well as vibrating through the bones.

In December, Alex also started listening to the iLs Sensory Motor program, with bone conduction, for a half hour a day, five days a week at home. He usually did activities from the iLs Playbook on the balancing disc. iLs provides pictures and directions of activities to perform, many of which take place on a balancing disc. In March, Alex began listening to the Concentration and Attention Focus Program, with bone conduction, twice a week, in my office. He usually listened to C&A for a half hour to forty-five minutes. Dad expressed that he really wanted to see more attention to details and directions by Alex.

With me, Alex does my usual variety of activities. With his mom, he usually does fifteen minutes of the balance disc and activities from the iLs Playbook, before he switches to LEGO. He says playing with LEGO helps him learn engineering skills.

Currently, Alex is working on Structure of Intellect (SOI) modules, the Belgau Platform and Rotation Boards, Brain Gym®, retained reflexes Brain Bag Exercises, Advanced Brain Training's Brain Builder, and other Brain Ways eclectic activities, as well as iLs.

Alex starts his day, every day, by doing Thinking Caps, Lion Yawns, 20 Active 8s, Brain Gym®–style, and a few minutes of the Cross Crawl. He lies on a swimming noodle on the floor and massages his spinal cord for two minutes to increase the fluid available in his brain each morning.

When Alex is with me for two hours a week, I try to match his "work" with what he seems willing to do. In that way, he gets plenty of movement but it's not a fight. When he is at Brain Ways, I emphasize the Structure of Intellect (SOI) modules, because I really mean it when I say we are going to activate and multiply neurons in his brain. Structure of Intellect builds those neurons. Alex is being challenged and is developing his aptitudes when he works in SOI. We work together on the paper booklets, where I watch and listen closely as he writes an answer, as I cannot always read it. I've taken to letting Alex use invisible ink sometimes, so he has to tell me what he is writing, as I cannot see it.

Alex also works on SOI on the computer. He is very computer savvy, so he will often choose this method, as it is easier than physically writing by hand for him. We just have to be sure we get some Cross Crawls, brain bag activities, or Belgau Board work in along with computer time, or he might choose to sit for a long time.

It was very helpful that Robert Meeker and Jody Brooks of SOI sent me some lower-level, easy booklets for Alex at the beginning. They surmised correctly that starting Alex at a less difficult level would build his confidence and let him know he could be successful. If he gets frustrated with a computer module, he'll take a break and work on some paper and pencil activities. Jody offered to "publish" Alex's Divergent production of seMantic Units (DMU) booklet when he finished his creative writing stories. Receiving that published book was a true highlight for Alex and me.

When Alex has trouble hitting the correct colors and numbers on the Visual Motor Control Stick (VMCS) on the Belgau Board, and his stick-to-it-iveness begins to dim, he'll ask if he can show me or the adult he is with how awesome he is on the computer module "Getting from Here to There." There are some times as many as thirteen lines joining the letters A to M, but Alex has developed his skill so that he can find the shortest path quickly in Level 3, which is the most difficult on the disc.

His mother and I are already noticing changes in Alex's behavior. In my office, he is showing more independence and less anger. He starts right to "work" without dilly-dallying. Homework, which used to be a nearly two-hour struggle, has been reduced to less than forty minutes—sometimes only twenty! His teachers have also noted positive changes in his academic work.

To augment Alex's physical activities, he has been teaching younger students at his school some of the activities, exercises, and songs from Brendan O'Hara's *Movement & Learning* CDs. The preschool teacher is very impressed as this fifth grader comes in and leads her young students in brain bag songs and activities twice a week. I went to observe and loved hearing the little ones asking questions of "Mr." Alex.

Alex's ability to jump on the trampoline has also greatly improved. He was hesitant to jump at first. He began jumping with straight legs, like a wooden soldier. He showed no rhythm. Now, Alex appears more comfortable and does not resist jumping. He is able to jump in the big-little-big-little sequence. His ability to jump to music and count or follow a rhythm is improving. His laterality calling, which is a vision therapy exercise where the jumper has to call out and show with hand motions the direction (up, down, left, or right) of the arrows on an 8x11 paper on the wall, is excellent. Alex can even look at the arrows and call out and move his hands the opposite direction of the four directions shown on the sheet. Those neural pathways are definitely opening.

Two years after I wrote the first part of this chapter, Alex continues to work with me. He is completing the Optimum music section from the iLs Playlist. He has completed the other three: Sensory Motor, Concentration and Attention, and Reading and Auditory Processing music. As I have written, all my clients listen to the music when they are working their vestibular and performing other exercises in my office. Alex is fun to watch, because he will often "get into" the music and start humming along or moving his arms like a conductor if it is a rousing piece. I believe he likes the music more than any of my clients. I give credit to the iLs for some of his gains, especially the sensory motor that he completed at home on a daily basis. I remember that the little six-year-old, Abbie, told her mother that she thought the music was making her happier; I think Alex is happier, too, when he is listening to the music.

Alex is also on his third CD filled with SOI modules. He has continued to progress in aptitudes, moving along to level three in many modules. Some of the modules give immediate feedback on the CD, which both of us appreciate. I know the underlying math and arithmetic aptitudes have been developing as his performance in school attests. His father wrote, "He struggles to express himself in language, but is finding that he can work with abstracts such as math and science with the right kind of support."

Alex is in middle school as of the revising of this book. Two main emphases working with him now are typing skills and that list of executive functions I worked on with Matthew:

- Getting organized
- Planning
- Initiating work
- Staying on task
- Controlling impulses
- Regulating emotions
- Being adaptable and resilient

I take great pleasure in seeing Alex's name on his paper, and his portfolio with all his papers organized by class. He is really maturing. He is growing into the list of executive functions as well as can be expected of a seventh grader. When we work on a topic, he is a willing listener and tries to complete the goals we set.

Typing has proved a challenge, but more than likely it is because Alex has used the "hunt and peck" system of typing on his computer for quite some time, so it is hard for him to stay within my "you must use your ring finger always for 's' and 'l'" rules. He is still motivated by LEGO, so I have purchased a couple of LEGO pieces as prizes for when he accomplishes our goals. He understands that typing can make life easier for him, as his handwriting is hindered by his tremor and the development of his fine motor skills, so I am hoping internal motivation is at work also.

Dad is overjoyed and enthusiastic that Alex is showing social skills that were not expected. Many ACC children have major difficulties in socializing generally and making friends specifically. Alex joined Boy Scouts and often tells me about the activities of his troop and how he is involved. Alex has a friend with whom he makes movies. I asked his parents to comment on his social development. Dad wrote, "Alex continues to show abilities that are on the high functioning end of the ACC spectrum of abilities. He is definitely challenged by standard schooling . . . but he is managing to stay mainstreamed (if sometimes with great difficulty and frustration on his part). He also continues to develop socially in ways that many ACC kids won't ever come remotely close to."

Another comment from his dad brought me back to the images of Alex trying to jump on a trampoline in our first months working together. It is hard to imagine that the wooden soldier with straight legs, arms at his sides, and absolutely no rhythm to his bounce can be this same child. Yet now, as his dad wrote, "he can get up and not just try different dances but enjoy taking part of them in the middle of a community of dancers because he identifies with them as his community."

I would like to show Alex's growth using some standardized testing, but he is not required to complete State Testing at school. He completed the WISC and Woodcock before I met him, but has not taken either again since I began working with him. Alex was unable to take the Auditory Processing test I use because he uses hearing aids for hearing loss. What I would really like to report is that his brain shows growth, too, but he has not had an MRI in the last three years, either. So, what I have to report is anecdotal and subjective: I think he has come a long way, baby; he is still working and going strong. As his dad wrote, "Yes, he's different from other kids but not so different that he can't interact with them and find a place there."

Glossary

Alignment. A skill to align each eye when looking at an object or performing a task. If the eyes do not line up together it can cause space judging problems, eye fatigue and strain, doubling of print, or movement of letters.

Amblyopia (also known as "lazy eye"). A common term used to describe a condition where one eye sees poorly, even with eyeglasses or contact lenses. The proper medical term for this condition is amblyopia. Amblyopia can develop in childhood due to an obstruction of vision within one eye due to injury or disease. There can be significant differences between the clearness of the images seen by each eye due to far-sightedness, nearsightedness, or astigmatism. In amblyopia, the clarity or alignment of the images from the two eyes is very different, and if the child sees double, the brain may begin to ignore the vision in one eye. The favored eye compensates for the "lazy eye," so the child with amblyopia may not be aware of the problem until the better eye is covered.

Acuity. Clarity of eyesight. It gives no information, however, on whether or not meaning is obtained from what is seen.

Binocular alignment or binocular vision. Vision in which both eyes are used synchronously to produce a single image (Editors of the American Heritage Dictionaries 1995). For example, reading demands accurate binocular vision. When a person's eyes do not aim at the same place accurately and simultaneously, he or she will have much more difficulty with large amounts of reading, writing, and other close work.

Convergence. Convergence is the coordinated movement and focus of our two eyes inward. Close work requires us to focus both of our eyes inward on close objects, including books, papers, computer screens, etc. Convergence skills are learned and developed during our early years.

Depth perception. This is the ability to see in 3-D. If both eyes work well and line up together then the brain will see objects in three dimensions.

Diplopia or double vision. This can result if our eyes do not both aim in the same place either at a distance or up close. The double images may be totally separate or overlap to some degree. Double vision can develop over time or appear suddenly.

Esotropia. See "strabismus."

Exotropia. Exotropia, commonly called wandering eye or wall-eye, is the visual condition in which a person uses only one eye to look at an object while the other eye turns outward. Exotropia is one of several types of strabismus, a condition resulting in eye turns or deviating eyes. This condition usually does not involve faulty or damaged eye muscles. Eye coordination may not be developed enough to provide normal control of the person's binocular vision. (See "strabismus.")

Flexibility. Ability to change focus between distant and near objects quickly and accurately.

Hypertropia. See "strabismus."

Hypotropia. See "strabismus."

Phoneme. The smallest unit of sound that gives meaning to a word.

Proprioceptive (from Integrated Listening Systems manual). The sense of one's own body—where it is, how to control it, how to move it—to the point where we don't need to think about it, comes from the receptors in our joints and muscles and is referred to as proprioception. This is an often-overlooked sensory system that contributes to behavior and the ability to learn. When this system is integrated with the other sensory systems, the brain is freed up to focus on higher order activities. Children and adults who improve their proprioceptive abilities are able to approach learning and communication tasks in a more relaxed and regulated manner.

Pursuit. Smooth pursuit eye movements allow the eyes to closely follow a moving object.

Reticular Activating System (RAS). The RAS is a network of neurons deep in the brainstem that receives input from all sensory systems. It sends nonspecific information to the brain to "wake it up." It is involved with regulating arousal and sleep-wake transitions, alertness, appropriate arousal to attend to the task at hand, and even prepares the motor system for action.

Saccades. Rapid, ballistic movements of the eyes that abruptly change the point of fixation (Purves et al. 2001).

Stereopsis/suppression 3-D/stereo vision. Stereo vision or stereopsis is also referred to as 3-D vision. Stereopsis—from stereo, meaning solidity, and opsis, meaning vision or sight—describes the sensation of depth attained from the successful merging of the two slightly different pictures seen in each eye into one 3-D image. The condition of stereo blindness occurs when two eyes do not work together to create one 3-D image. (From COVD website.)

Strabismus. Misaligned eyes or crossed eyes. The inability to point both eyes in the same direction at the same time. One eye may appear to turn in (esotropia), out (exotropia), up (hypertropia), or down (hypotropia). The eye turn may occur constantly or only intermittently. Eye-turning may change from one eye to the other, and may only appear when a person is tired or has done a lot of reading. Strabismus may cause double vision.

Tracking. Term applied to a function of eye movement abilities, which are also known as "oculomotor function." It refers to the ability to quickly and accurately look (fixate), visually follow a moving object (pursuit), and efficiently move our eyes so we can fixate on objects from point to point as in reading (saccades) (Fortenbacher 2010).

Vectograms. Polarized slides that vision therapists can use with patients to practice vergence, suppression, and many activities to improve a variety of skills.

Vestibular. Directly connected to the cochlea of the inner ear, the vestibular system is responsible for balance, coordination, muscle tone, rhythm, and awareness of the body in space. It plays a key role in organizing motor output and posture. The vestibular system, along with proprioceptive inputs, also has a strong impact on attention and emotional regulation. Once these systems are functioning well, we are better able to participate in higher brain functions such as reading, writing, and expressive language.

VESTIBULAR APPARATUS

⊙ Vestibular apparatus and cochlea form the inner ear

⊙ Vestibular apparatus— provides sense of equilibrium
  • consists of otolith organs (utricle and saccule) and semicircular canals

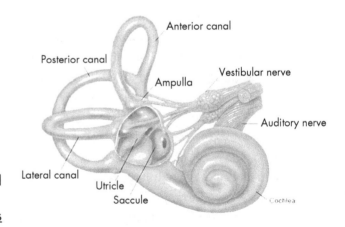

Anterior canal

Posterior canal

Vestibular nerve

Ampulla

Auditory nerve

Lateral canal

Utricle

Saccule

Cochlea

Bibliography

Adamec, Christine A. *Moms with ADD: A Self-help Manual*. Dallas, TX: Taylor Pub., 2000.

Amen, Daniel G. *Healing ADD: The Breakthrough Program That Allows You to See and Heal the Six Types of Attention Deficit Disorder*. New York: G.P. Putnam's Sons, 2001.

Arrowsmith-Young, Barbara. *The Woman Who Changed Her Brain: And Other Inspiring Stories of Pioneering Brain Transformation*. New York City: Free Press, 2012.

Assessing Reading: Multiple Measures for Kindergarten through Twelfth Grade. Novato, CA: Arena Press, 2008.

Ayres, A. Jean, and Jeff Robbins. *Sensory Integration and the Child*. Los Angeles, CA: Western Psychological Services, 1979.

Ball, Ron. *Freedom at Your Fingertips: Get Rapid Physical and Emotional Relief with the Breakthrough System of Tapping*. Fredericksburg, VA: Inroads Publishing, 2011.

Ballinger, Erich. *The Learning Gym: Fun-to-Do Activities for Success at School*. Ventura, CA: Edu-Kinesthetics, Inc., 2004.

Barhydt, Elizabeth, and Hamilton "Hap" Barhydt, PhD. *Self-Help For Kids, Improving Performance And Building Self-Esteem*. Groveland, CA: Loving Life, 1995.

Barry, Susan R. *Fixing My Gaze: A Scientist's Journey into Seeing in Three Dimensions*. New York: Basic Books, 2010.

Batchelor, Phil. *Raising Parents: Nine Powerful Principles*. Martinez, CA: Phil Batchelor, 1988.

Bayard, Robert Thomas, and Jean Bayard. *How to Deal with Your Acting-up Teenager: Practical Self-Help for Desperate Parents*. New York: M. Evans & Company, Inc., 1983.

Begley, Sharon. *Train Your Mind, Change Your Brain: How a New Science Reveals Our Extraordinary Potential to Transform Ourselves*. New York: Ballantine Books, 2007.

Belgau, Beverly, and Frank Belgau. Personal conversations, 2016.

Belgau, Frank A., PhD. *The Pendulum Ball*. Port Angeles, WA 2001.

Belgau, Frank A., PhD. *Visual Motor Control Stick and Pendulum Ball*. Port Angeles, WA, 2001.

Benoit, Robin, and Jillian Benoit. *Jillian's Story: How Vision Therapy Changed My Daughter's Life*. Dallas, TX: P3 Press, 2010.

Biel, Lindsey. *Raising a Sensory Smart Child*. New York: Penguin Press, 2009.

Birnbaum, M., K. Koslowe, and R. Sanet. "Success in amblyopia therapy as a function of age: a literature survey." *American Journal of Optometry and Physiological Optics* 54 (1977): 269–75.

Coulter, Rachel A. "Understanding the visual symptoms of individuals with autism spectrum disorder (ASD)." Optom Vis Dev 2009, 40 (3): 164-175.

Covey, Stephen R., A. Roger Merrill, and Rebecca R. Merrill. *First Things First: To Live, to Love, to Learn, to Leave a Legacy.* New York: Simon & Schuster, 1994.

Cox, Adam J. *No Mind Left Behind: Understanding and Fostering Executive Control—the Eight Essential Brain Skills Every Child Needs to Thrive.* New York: Perigee Book/Penguin Group, 2007.

Davis, Ronald D., and Eldon M. Braun. *The Gift of Dyslexia: Why Some of the Smartest People Can't Read and How They Can Learn.* New York: Berkley Pub. Group, 1997.

Davis, Ronald D., and Eldon M. Braun. *The Gift of Learning: Proven New Methods for Correcting ADD, Math & Handwriting Problems.* New York: Berkley Pub. Group, 2003.

Dawson, Peg, and Richard Guare. *Smart but Scattered: The Revolutionary "Executive Skills" Approach to Helping Kids Reach Their Potential.* New York: Guilford Press, 2009.

Dennison, Gail E., Paul E. Dennison, and Jerry Teplitz. *Brain Gym® for Business: Instant Brain Boosters for On-the-job Success.* Ventura, CA: Edu-Kinesthetics, 2004.

Dennison, Paul E., and Gail Dennison. *Edu-K for Kids: The Basic Manual on Educational Kinesiology for Parents & Teachers of Kids of All Ages!* Ventura, CA: Edu-Kinesthetics, 1987.

Dennison, Paul E., and Gail E. Dennison. *Brain Gym®: Teacher's Edition.* Ventura, CA: Hearts at Play, 2010.

Dennison, Paul E., and Gail E. Dennison. *Personalized Whole Brain Integration.* Ventura, CA: Edu-Kinesthetics, Inc. 1985.

Doidge, Norman. *The Brain That Changes Itself: Stories of Personal Triumph from the Frontiers of Brain Science.* New York: Viking, 2007.

Doman, G. Alexander. *The Listening Program Level One Kit Guidebook.* Ogden, Utah: Advanced Brain Technologies, 2006.

Eagleman, David. *Incognito: The Secret Lives of the Brain.* New York: Vintage Books, 2012.

Editors of the American Heritage Dictionaries. *The American Heritage Stedman's Medical Dictionary.* Boston: Houghton Mifflin, 1995.

Exkorn, Karen Siff. *The Autism Sourcebook: Everything You Need to Know About Diagnosis, Treatment, Coping and Healing.* New York: HarperCollins, 2005.

Flach, Frederic. *Rickie.* New York: Fawcett Columbine, 1990.

Friends in Recovery. *The Twelve Steps: A Key to Living with Attention Deficit Disorder.* San Diego: RPI Pub., 1996.

Gates, Tanner. "Dynamic Vision: Vision Therapy through the Anti-Gravity System." *Journal of Behavioral Optometry,* Vol. 23, Issue 2, 2012.

Goddard, Sally. *Reflexes, Learning and Behavior: A Window Into the Child's Mind.* Eugene: Fern Ridge Press, 2005.

Granet, D.B., C.F. Gomi, R. Ventura, and A. Miller-Scholte. "The Relationship between Convergence Insufficiency and ADHD." *Strabismus* 13 no. 4 (2005):163–8.

Hallowell, Edward M., and John J. Ratey. *Driven to Distraction: Recognizing and Coping with Attention Deficit Disorder from Childhood through Adulthood.* New York: Simon & Schuster, 1995.

Hannaford, Carla. *The Dominance Factor: How Knowing Your Dominant Eye, Ear, Brain, Hand & Foot Can Improve Your Learning.* Arlington, VA: Great Ocean Publishers, 1997.

Hannaford, Carla. *Smart Moves: Why Learning Is Not All in Your Head.* Arlington, VA: Great Ocean Publishers, 1995.

Hartmann, Thom. *Healing ADD: Simple Exercises That Will Change Your Daily Life.* Grass Valley, CA: Underwood Books, 1998.

Hartmann, Thom. *Thom Hartmann's Complete Guide to ADHD: Help for Your Family at Home, School, and Work.* Grass Valley, CA: Underwood Books, 2000.

Hengber, Elizabeth, Mike Post, and Brian Nash. *The Power of One.* Milwaukee, WI: Hal Leonard Corp., 2007.

Hoban, Tana. *Black & White.* New York: HarperCollins Children's Books, 2007.

Hoban, Tana. *Black on White.* New York: HarperCollins Children's Books, 1993.

Isay, Jane. *Walking on Eggshells: Navigating the Delicate Relationship between Adult Children and Their Parents.* New York: Broadway Books/Flying Dolphin Press, 2008.

Jensen, Eric. *Teaching with the Brain in Mind.* Alexandria, VA: Association for Supervision and Curriculum Development, 2005.

Kelly, Kate, and Peggy Ramundo. *You Mean I'm Not Lazy, Stupid or Crazy?!: A Self-Help Book for Adults with Attention Deficit Disorder.* New York: Simon & Schuster, 1996.

Kranowitz, Carol Stock. *The Out-of-Sync Child: Recognizing and Coping with Sensory Processing Disorder.* New York: Skylight Press Book/A Perigee Book, 2005.

Kratky, Lada Josefa, *Cancionero! Big Book of Songs, Level A.* Carmel, CA: Hampton Brown, 1996.

Krebs, Charles, PhD. *A Revolutionary Way of Thinking: From a Near-Fatal Accident to a New Science of Healing.* Melbourne: Hill of Content, 1998.

Krebs, Charles T. *Nutrition for the Brain: Feeding Your Brain for Optimal Mental Performance.* South Yarra, Victoria: Michelle Anderson Publishing, 2006.

Kupfer, Carl. "Treatment of Amblyopia Ex Anopsia in Adults." *American Journal of Opthamology* 43 no. 6 (1957): 918–22.

Lane, Kenneth A., OD, FCOVD. *Developing Ocular Motor and Visual Perceptual Skills: An Activity Action Guide.* Thorofare, New Jersey: Slack Incorporated, 2005.

Lane, Kenneth A., OD, FCOVD. *Developing Your Child for Success.* Lewisville, Texas: Learning Potentials Publishers, Inc., 1991.

Lane, Sarah, and Michael Cron, Drs. College of Optometrists in Vision Development's Website. https://cordblog.wordpress.com/2106/03/08/the-spectrum-of-autism.

Linenthal, Peter. *Look. Look!* New York: Dutton Children's Books, 1998.

Maino D.M., S.G. Viola, and R. Donati. "The Etiology of Autism." *Optometry & Vision Development* 40 no. 3 (2009): 150–156.

Meeker, Mary N., Ed.D., *An interpretation guide with strategies for using SOI: Interpreting and using SOI test results.* Springfield, OR: SOI Systems,1992.

Meeker, Mary N., Ed.D., and Robert Meeker, Ed.D., "What Is SOI?" M&M Systems, Springfield, Oregon, 1978.

Robert Meeker, Ed.D., SOI Vision from M&M Systems, 2007.

Nelsen, Jane. *Positive Discipline.* New York: Ballantine Books, 1987.

O'Hara, Brendan. *Movement & Learning, Beanbag Ditties.* Australia: Brendan O'Hara, 2003.

O'Hara, Brendan. *Movement & Learning, The Children's Song Book.* Brendan O'Hara, 1991a.

O'Hara, Brendan. *Movement & Learning, Wombat & His Mates Song Book.* Brendan O'Hara, 1991b.

O'Hara, Brendan. *Primitive and Postural Reflexes Didgeridoo and Beanbags.* Durham, 2004.

O'Hara, Brendan. Private Conversation, 2017.

Promislow, Sharon. *Making the Brain/Body Connection: A Playful Guide to Releasing Mental, Physical & Emotional Blocks to Success.* West Vancouver, B.C.: Kinetic Pub., 1998.

Purves, Dale, George J. Augustine, David Fitzpatrick, Lawrence C. Katz, Anthony-Samuel Lamantia, Jomes O. McNamara, and S. Mark Williams. *Neuroscience.* Sunderland, MA: Sinauer Associates, Inc., 2001.

Ricker, Audrey, and Carolyn Crowder. *Backtalk: Four Steps to Ending Rude Behavior in Your Kids.* New York: Simon & Schuster, 1998.

Riley, Douglas. *The Defiant Child: A Parent's Guide to Oppositional Defiant Disorder.* Dallas, TX: Taylor Pub., 1997.

Sanet, Linda, and Robert Sanet. Vision Therapy Workshop, 2013.

Siegel, Daniel J., MD, and Tina Payne Bryson, PhD. *The Whole-Brain Child: 12 Revolutionary Strategies to Nurture Your Child's Developing Mind*. New York: Bantam Books Trade Paperbacks, 2012.

Silverman, Linda Kreger. *Upside-Down Brilliance: The Visual-Spatial Learner*. Denver, CO: DeLeon Pub., 2002.

Solden, Sari. *Journeys through ADDulthood: Discover a New Sense of Identity and Meaning While Living with Attention Deficit Disorder*. New York: Walker & Company, 2002.

Tolle, Eckhart. *The Power of Now*. Novato, CA: New World Library, 1999.

Index

Acknowledgments

TO THE BEAUTIFUL, HELPFUL CHILDREN who posed for this book's pictures, I give my thanks. Each one was a pleasure to work with. Many of my previous clients are now in university and beyond, so I recruited models from a talented group in and near Alameda, California: Abby Gorin, Alex Batty, Colin Pero, Dominic Marble, Finn Thornton, Flora Smith, Gino Marble, Jack Thornton, Jacob Morgan, Justin Williams-Huhn, Kate West, Katelynn Hernandez, Levi Pero, Matt Thornton, Maya Fong, Meg Rosenbaum, Niyani Martin, Virginia Morgan, and Zachary Siskind.

To Alain McLaughlin, the fabulous photographer who took the pictures of the models with sincere joy, this book is more readable for his every "picture that speaks a thousand words."

My best friend from seventh grade, Cindy Walton Solberg, became my first editor, going through each chapter with her teacher-principal-editor red pen and giving me much-needed feedback. I am so appreciative of Cindy's efforts and glad we can share in the book's publication.

I acknowledge Dr. Jay Scott Neale, D.D., RscD., Tri-City Religious Science Center, who when I asked him early on in my own writing process how he had managed to write books, told me that he emulated the author Stephen King, who wrote two hours a day. I tried to follow Dr. Jay's advice, and here is the book!

I remember the words of Larhken Carroll and Pam Whitman who both told me always to do some Brain Gym exercises each time I sat down to write. I followed their advice, too, and was glad for it.

I am happy I asked Brooke Warner, of Warner Coaching, to coach me through the publishing process. She is a true professional and shared her wisdom and know-how with me.

Annie Tucker is such a personable, hardworking editor. I feel blessed that she worked as my developmental editor. She reorganized my chapters, making them much easier to read, as well as helping me to get my points across.

For the graphics, I am so glad Teryn Brown showed me what a graphic artist can do. Thanks to other graphic contributors as well: Sarah Graff, Brendan O'Hara, and Rachel Thompson.

For the copyedit, I thank Krissa Lagos, who read through the entire manuscript, taking out repeated passages and revising unclear ones.

I love the cover of *The Fantastic Elastic Brain* and hope you do, too. Kudos to Tabitha Lahr for taking my ideas and making a cover that stands out. She also designed the book's interior, working meticulously on the layout of the photos and graphics, as well as choosing the fonts.

To the doctors, staff, and patients at Larkspur Landing Optometry—my fellow vision therapy specialist and friend, Keiko Vaughan; the indispensable April Anderson and the always-helpful Sarah Hendrix, Dr. Gina Day, and Dr. Jaime Hatanaka—I thank you. Thanks also to those patients whose stories were edited out but who contributed greatly to my knowledge of how vision therapy changes lives: Sebas, Dakota, Scarlett, Tricia, Max, Donovan, Abby, Olivier, and so many more I cannot name them all.

To the parents of all my Brain Ways kids, thanks for transporting your children to my office, especially though Guatemalan traffic—and a special shout out to my neighbor Daniela Giesemann Morel, too, for logistics.

To Touch for Health experts, Arlene Green and Larry Green who provided the explanation of muscle testing for the book, and Matthew Thie, for teaching me muscle testing and balancing as well as explaining the meridians, chakras and the energy within the body.

To Lucia Asensio Feucht, without whom there would not have been many stories.

To Tirra Stenstedt for her friendship.

To Christian Storm, Kiyomi Miller, and Vincent Bolentini for their IT expertise.

And, to my daughter, Lisa, who shared our time together with the book.

About the Author

BETSY SCHOOLEY is the creator and director of Brain Ways, a neuro-plasticity-focused, one-on-one program consisting of exercises designed to stimulate learners' new neuron and neural pathway development. Predicated on the idea that "neurons that fire together wire together," Brain Ways was inspired by Betsy's desire to find ways to help students like those who she had seen struggling in traditional classroom environments.

Betsy has a lifetime California K-9 teaching credential, as well as Spanish bilingual and language development specialist certificates. Her teaching career spanned thirty years, mostly in the California Bay Area as well as in Guatemala City, Boston, and Champaign, Illinois. Since 2009, Betsy has helped many children improve their visual skills and reading through her work as a vision therapist and her collaboration with the Gemstone Foundation on Dynamic Vision Training/DVT school projects.

Betsy lives in Alameda, California, and plays doubles tennis, pickleball, and Liar's Dice for fun. She also sings in the Douglas Morrisson Theatre Chorus. *The Fantastic Elastic Brain* is her first book.

Author photo © Alain McLaughlin